"I loved this book! You don't f one. On each page Kevin offers practical insight and a wonderful ability to communicate hope for your marriage. This book is worth your investment of time. Great insight and life-changing principles."

Jim Burns, PhD, president, HomeWord;
author of *Creating an Intimate Marriage*, *Closer*,
The First Few Years of Marriage, and
Getting Ready for Marriage

"In his new book, *Happily: 8 Commitments of Couples Who Laugh, Love & Last*, Kevin A. Thompson has written an excellent guide to help couples achieve a happy, loving, and joyful marriage. Filled with interesting insights and powerful wisdom, it keeps readers turning page after page. Curl up in a comfy chair with a blanket and a cup of coffee—you're going to love this one!"

Rick Johnson, bestselling author
of *Becoming Your Spouse's Better Half*
and *How to Talk So Your Husband Will Listen*

"Certainly, marriage is no fairy tale. But it can be full of laughter and love, and Kevin uses his insight and experience to describe actionable ways we can live out the commitments of the Beatitudes in the day-to-day of marriage. Having witnessed his relationship with his wife, Jenny, firsthand, I find it refreshing to read an honest account of the work and the fun involved in making a relationship not only work but last. There will always be stumbles on the path one walks with their spouse, but Kevin and his wife navigate them with practicality, humility, and a healthy dose of humor. I thoroughly enjoyed this book and look forward to putting it to good use in my own marriage."

Kristan Roland, blogger, *Confessions of a Cookbook Queen*

"Marriage is not simply luck; it is a series of wise choices that make up the path to the happily ever after. At the beginning of our Love-Wise ministry, we made a commitment to help couples gain the how-tos that make for healthy relationships. In *Happily: 8 Commitments of Couples Who Laugh, Love & Last*, Pastor Kevin A. Thompson has created a practical, doable, and helpful road map so every willing couple can journey successfully to a love that lasts—happily!"

Pam and Bill Farrel, authors of forty-five books, including the bestselling *Men Are Like Waffles, Women Are Like Spaghetti* and *Red Hot Monogamy*

HAPPILY

Books by Kevin Thompson

Friends, Partners, and Lovers
Happily

HAPPILY

8 COMMITMENTS OF COUPLES WHO
LAUGH, LOVE & LAST

KEVIN A. THOMPSON

Revell

a division of Baker Publishing Group
Grand Rapids, Michigan

© 2018 by Kevin A. Thompson

Published by Revell
a division of Baker Publishing Group
PO Box 6287, Grand Rapids, MI 49516-6287
www.revellbooks.com

Printed in the United States of America

Library of Congress Cataloging-in-Publication Data
Names: Thompson, Kevin A., author.
Title: Happily : 8 commitments of couples who laugh, love, and last / Kevin A. Thompson.
Description: Grand Rapids : Revell-Baker Publishing Group, 2018. | Includes bibliographical references and index.
Identifiers: LCCN 2018014356 | ISBN 9780800728120 (pbk. : alk. paper)
Subjects: LCSH: Marriage—Religious aspects—Christianity.
Classification: LCC BV835 .T4925 2018 | DDC 248.8/44—dc23
LC record available at https://lccn.loc.gov/2018014356

The author is represented by the William K. Jensen Literary Agency.

18 19 20 21 22 23 24   7 6 5 4 3 2 1

In memory of Bruce Palmer
and in honor of Verna Palmer,
who faithfully modeled these commitments
to one another

And to Jenny, whom I happily call my own

CONTENTS

Contents

ACKNOWLEDGMENTS

This is what I always dreamed writing would be like. I'm eight hundred miles from home in a cabin in Colorado. To my right is a fire occasionally inviting me to come sit by it for its warmth. To my left the snow is covering the grass on the riverbank as the water gently rolls downstream.

Today is a negotiated outcome. I wanted a few days to look at the manuscript in the midst of peace and quiet. Jenny wanted our kids to experience the ski slopes while they were still young enough to learn them quickly. As we try to do, we made both happen. As my wife and her siblings chase our kids and nieces and nephews around the slopes, I reread this manuscript, considering the suggestions of wise editors and reflecting on my marriage.

While these acknowledgments may have been written in the quiet of Colorado's early spring, this book was written in the chaos of career and family—Jenny's marketing company, two energetic kids beginning a transition to middle school, writing and speaking engagements, and pastoring a church full of people who invite me into the happiest and saddest days of their lives. I often joke with Jenny that during this season I long for the day when I will get to write in peace and quiet, but I'll bet if that season ever comes I'll long to go back to the days when I would yell at my kids, "Be quiet, I've got to finish this article on good parenting."

Thank you, Ella and Silas. You have made sacrifices so your father could write. I hope not too many. I've desperately tried to get it right—to push aside the computer to go play catch or to close the manuscript in order to listen to what you've had to say. But I know I've missed the mark on occasions. I've enjoyed this season of parenting and pray you look back on these years with great fondness.

Thank you to those who encouraged me to write and to those who made my writing better. To readers of www.kevin athompson.com, whose experiences help me understand the need. To family and friends—those who live on the compound and those who just come to visit. To the leadership, staff, and membership of Community Bible Church. To Andrea and her team at Revell as well as Teresa and those at the William K. Jensen Literary Agency.

But most of all, to Jenny. As I reread the words in this manuscript, I'm reminded of how well you live them out. With an amazing consistency you model for me and our kids how a wife and mom is supposed to love. I don't just love you, I'm happily in love with you.

INTRODUCTION

More Than Luck

It's unmistakable. Blindfold me, take me into five different fast-food restaurants, make me order a Number 1, and just in the interaction with the cashier I can tell you whether or not we are at a Chick-fil-A. It's not the sounds or smells. At each restaurant, the ordering and paying processes are the same. The signal of where we are is not in what the employee does. It's how they do it.

Chick-fil-A is notorious for training and paying their employees to be nice. Ask them for anything and they will respond, "My pleasure." While clearly not everything a fast-food employee is asked to do is their pleasure, they say it anyway. And almost without exception, the customer believes it.

We are a society fixated on the *whats* of life. What does a company do to get a competitive advantage? What does a team do to prepare for the big game? What did you do to get your last promotion? What does a couple need to do to have a happy marriage? The whats matter in business, sports, work, marriage, and life. They matter so much that my first marriage book, *Friends, Partners, and Lovers*, was a book about the whats of marriage. What does a happy couple do? They build their friendship, partnership, and intimacy.

But just as important as the whats in life are the *hows*. How do you do business? How does your team approach practice or a game? How will you and your spouse act in marriage? Chick-fil-A wants their employees to approach their work like a privilege. This privilege is displayed by their pleasure of serving.

This is a book about the hows of relationships. As husbands and wives go about their daily lives, a certain attitude should follow them wherever they go. The whats of a healthy marriage will be done happily.

Happily is an adverb, and adverbs are often used to describe verbs. While the verbs are the action words, adverbs can describe the manner in which those verbs occur. A good marriage is full of verbs. Whenever I officiate at a wedding ceremony, I have the couple vow five verbs to God, their families, and one another—love, care, listen, learn, and be one with. But marriage has many more verbs than that— forgive, trust, submit, encourage, cheer, wait, embrace, etc. The verbs describe what a couple does in a marriage, but the adverb *happily* reveals the manner in which those actions should be done.

Happiness was never intended to be the main focus of marriage. Gary Thomas is right when he asks in the subtitle of *Sacred Marriage*, "What if God designed marriage to make us holy more than to make us happy?" Happiness is not the central focus and should not be the central pursuit of a couple. When it is the focus, it's rarely experienced. Happiness is a by-product. When we pursue it, we don't find it. Yet when a couple chooses rightly and lives wisely, happiness comes along for the ride.

When happiness is not a general description of a couple's relationship, something is wrong. Clearly there are bad seasons—not just days, but weeks and months—but the overarching feeling of a husband and wife should be one that life is better together than apart. They should be happily married to one another.

Recently I was sitting down with a friend, who told me his wife had cheated on him. The news was shocking to him, but not to me. The life-altering news my friend had just received is experienced on a nearly daily basis even in our small town.

He couldn't fathom why she had done it. Little did he know it was as predictable as any relationship struggle could be. He had been clueless for years. Moments of struggle had come, but they seemed normal. He reached out for help one time, but before any help was given the issue passed. He thought everything was fine.

Her heart had been dying for years. His ignorance and apathy had been blind to the slow death. Mesmerized by career and hobbies, confusing the birth of children with the certainty of love, he couldn't see what was right before him. Aware of every nuance of emotion in a potential sale, he never noticed his wife no longer smiled, laughed, or spoke about the future.

"I can't believe she did this," he kept repeating.

I can't believe she waited to do this, I kept thinking.

Poor choices should never be excused, but they are often easy to understand. Having died a slow death, her heart was looking for anything or anyone that could bring it back to life. An innocent Facebook comment led to an inbox message and ended in a six-month affair.

He wanted to get help; she wanted to get out. The odds of success were against them. Despite hundreds of text messages, many phone calls, and some of the most uncomfortable face-to-face conversations one can imagine, it wouldn't be long before another family would be broken apart—the husband thinking she killed a good thing, the wife thinking the "good thing" had ended long ago.

It is not a unique story. According to the Centers for Disease Control and Prevention, a woman has only a 52 percent chance of her first marriage making it to the twentieth anniversary.[1] Maybe the greatest proof that something is wrong with marriage is the need for the Centers for Disease Control and Prevention to publish such statistics. The numbers might prove a point, but few people need it proved.

Marriages are struggling. We see the evidence in workplaces, where men and women are sending out messages of their hurting hearts, looking for anyone to recognize them and connect with them. The struggle is felt through social media, as boundaries are dropped and old relationships are rekindled. The heartbreak is obvious in the saddened eyes of school children, who know whichever parent picks them up is the only parent they will see that night. We hear the sorrow of these marriages in conversations with our friends, we deal with the chaos in our families, and often we know the tension exists in our own marriages.

Divorce is contagious. It spreads through peer groups with such speed everyone assumes it's unavoidable. It appears inevitable, as though it's not a matter of *if* as much as *when*. It can become overwhelming, an almost self-fulfilling prophecy. The brokenness is all around us.

In contrast, I think about my grandparents, happily married seventy years. It's easy to look at their marriage and say, "They are lucky."

Yet nothing appeared lucky about their original circumstances. They were born in poverty and at a time where childbirth was far more dangerous than any modern threat, married at an age that we would now consider far too young, cast from home into military service, driven less by love of country and more by hatred of farming, separated by the ocean during several wars, struggling to raise children on a staff sergeant's salary. Plenty of others seemed to have an advantage in life.

But they *were* the lucky ones—one partner for one life that has stretched into the ninth decade. A few wars, a few children, and a lifetime of little income never seemed to cast any doubt on their love. Search for a bad word, and one was never spoken. Search for an out-of-bounds topic of conversation because it might bring up a bad memory, and one could never be found. "Blessed," they would say. "Lucky," we would all claim.

The plight of so many broken marriages feels like a curse, as if there is a marriage-eating virus that can move unseen onto unsuspecting couples, destroying their commitments and love with a speed that can't even compare to the speed at which we can fall in love.

Divorce feels like a curse for which there is no control and no cure. But feelings are deceiving. There is influence and control. A broken ending is not a guarantee. Marriages that end quickly have actually been decaying for months or years.

Small decisions and behaviors go unseen, slowly destroying the foundation of a healthy relationship.

A good marriage feels like luck—like we have struck the jackpot. The word *happy* is rooted in the concept of chance. *Hap* can be used in *happy*, but it's also present in words like *happenstance* or *perhaps*. Being happy is so great that it feels as though it's a stroke of good fortune. Yet happiness is not happenstance. Good marriages do not face less conflict or difficulties; they aren't assured by great circumstances. Two couples can seemingly have the same income, the same experience, and the same circumstances and have radically different marriages. Why do some marriages work and others do not? Who are the lucky ones?

Luck is a term we use in a variety of situations. At times it describes an unlikely event. If one in a thousand people get a specific disease and we happen to be that one, we are just unlucky. Chances were that it wouldn't happen, but it did. There isn't a logical explanation. There was nothing we could have done differently. Some things in life are outside of our control, and we often attribute those things to luck.

At other times we use *luck* to describe skills we can't see. On the surface there is no reason our friend continually experiences success in the stock market while we have a long track record of mistiming the market or picking the one company in an industry that doesn't make money. We attribute to luck the co-worker who shows a pattern of success despite no obvious advantages in knowledge or ability. We say an opponent is lucky even though they continually have our number.

We often say something is lucky when we can't see—or don't want to see—the hidden skills another person possesses. When we look at an individual situation, calling something lucky is appropriate.

As someone who plays golf, I've witnessed about a dozen holes-in-one during my life, but two stand out. They were horrible shots. My dad skulled a ball four feet off the ground for 150 yards until it hit the flagstick and fell in. Another time a friend of mine hit the worst slice imaginable; the ball barely cleared a bunker, then bounced dead right and into the hole. And though every hole-in-one contains an element of luck, if you consistently hit good shots, you are far more likely to have that experience than if you never hit the ball near the green. A pattern of practice over time develops skill.

So it is with marriage. In a world full of broken relationships, it's easy to look at marriage like the flip of a coin. If it works, you were lucky. If it doesn't, you were unlucky, and there is nothing you can do about it.

It's true that any single relationship *can* feel like chance. Yet we're foolish to look at marriage on the whole as a simple luck of the draw. When there is a pattern of divorce, both individually and in society, that's not simply a run of bad luck. When many people have found meaningful relationships that last through the seasons of life, what they have experienced is more than just a good run.

The Modern Rules for Marriage

When couples come to see me, it's clear that though the modern rules for marriage are unspoken, they are clearly defined. The rules go something like this:

1. There is someone just for you. If you find them, you will have great success. If you don't, your relationship will struggle. Marriage is a flip of the coin regarding whether or not you have found your soul mate.

2. Run from pain. Ignore it, deny it, and do whatever you can to distance yourself from it. You aren't strong enough to endure hurt, sorrow, or grief. If you allow it near you, it might never leave. Marriage is fragile, so your relationship can't endure hardship. Deny unmet desires, push aside disappointments, and never talk about what you really want so you won't have to consider if you are happy or not.

3. When issues arise, either avoid or attack. More often than not, do both. When you experience disagreements or frustrations, pretend like everything is okay. Let things build until you finally explode. Then make your feelings unmistakably clear. Force your spouse to buckle under the weight of your emotion.

4. Never forget marriage is primarily about you: your own happiness, meaning, and satisfaction. For as long as you are happy in your relationship, support your spouse. But the moment your happiness wanes, consider if someone else can bring you more satisfaction. In all things, follow your heart as the ultimate guide.

5. There's no need for you to work at this relationship. A good marriage should happen naturally. Just based on what you've seen, what you know, and what you think to be right, you should be able to experience success. When problems arise, it shows there is either something wrong with your spouse or something broken with the institution of marriage.

6. Be careful with love and forgiveness. It's a scary world, so you should do everything you can to protect your heart. The best way for this to happen is to give only parts of yourself to people. When they have proven themselves trustworthy, give them access to an aspect of you, but never all of you. Make sure you are always hiding the parts of yourself that might cause them not to love you or that you don't want to be seen.

7. If you truly love each other, you'll always agree. You will instinctively know what the other is thinking. There isn't even a need to ask. You can assume you understand your partner and they understand you. Differing perspectives or conclusions may indicate that something is wrong in the relationship. Tension is not normally a characteristic of a truly good relationship. If your spouse can't read your mind, something is wrong with them.

8. When marriage is right, it should be easy. Others should applaud you. Friends and family should support you. Both internally and externally, everything should escort you toward a better relationship. If a friend disagrees or judges your relationship, it's a sign that something is wrong with the marriage. If something is right, it shouldn't be hard.

On nearly a monthly basis, I stand before a young couple as they commit their lives solely to one another. With rare exception the moment is full of great hope, as the couple is deeply in love. Despite their love and their freedom to willfully choose whom they will marry, nearly every couple communicates a nervousness of divorce before the wedding.

On the Saturdays I'm not standing in front of a young couple, I'm often standing before a more mature couple. Having experienced the sorrow of a broken marriage, they have chosen anyway to give marriage another try. Even as they state their vows, they often feel the outcome of their marriage is beyond their control.

The sense of helplessness from both the young and the old does not match the biblical concept of marriage. We are not helpless victims in this world. While we are fallen people who live in a fallen world and can suffer tremendous tragedies through no fault of our own, in many areas in our lives, the outcomes we face are determined by the choices we make. Generally speaking, good choices lead to good outcomes and bad choices lead to bad outcomes.

Without question, one person can destroy a marriage. However, even that person's decisions are not made in a vacuum but in correlation with the actions of their spouse. The good news that can be told to any couple is: if you make good choices, chances are your marriage will be a tremendous blessing to yourself and others. Yet within that truth is bad news—humanity rarely makes good choices.

If we choose wisely within marriage, our relationship will flourish. But what are wise choices? How do we make marriage work? Left to ourselves, we act based on our past experiences, a guess, or some hunch we've gotten from somewhere. It's the equivalent of saying, "You will be happy if you live in Switzerland," but then not being given a map to know where Switzerland is.

Most husbands and wives are going through marriage with no clue of how to be successful. Some marriages work and some don't. A few get lucky, but many spouses suffer unhappily for years, either enduring a lifeless relationship or suffering through the heartache of divorce.

It doesn't have to be this way. We don't have to be left to a marriage roulette where the smart money always bets against an enduring relationship.

There is a better way. There is a map to Switzerland. The map doesn't guarantee success; it doesn't mean a couple won't face a sorrow beyond their control that might destroy the relationship. But a map does exist that can make marriages last and turn lifeless relationships into fountains of comfort and meaning.

What We Want from Marriage

Expectations between two people are rarely the same. We all want different things when it comes to marriage, but while our desires may be nuanced, they probably aren't as unique as we think. If I could assure every couple I marry that they will have a relationship that is both fun and defined by a deep and abiding affection for one another, and that no matter what they might face, love will endure through even the toughest times, I believe every couple would sign on the dotted line. This is what we desire.

We Want to Laugh

Life is hard, and marriage will have its moments of difficulties. However, it should also be fun. If life doesn't have the promise of being more enjoyable with another person, few of us would make the commitment. Obviously situations and circumstances can arise where laughter doesn't describe a couple's relationship, but those should be the outliers. Laughter should be a regular part of our lives.

Some of my favorite moments of marriage are the times of laughter between me and my wife, Jenny. There are stories only we know about that cause us to laugh. The stress of parenting is often lightened as we keep a straight face with our kids but then laugh hysterically with one another over what they have said or done. Few things connect us like laughing together, whether it be in response to a comedian's tale or a crazy situation even taking place in our daily lives. Laughter is meant to be a central aspect of marriage.

We Want to Love

It might begin with passionate feelings of attraction or romance, but as a marriage matures, a couple's understanding of love deepens. Yes, we want passion, but men and women also desire the security and peace that derives from true love. There is a consistency and trust in real love.

Life can feel like a trapeze act. Before we are fully trained, we are expected to perform a bunch of tricks that require us to swing, fly, and flip. Marriage should cause us to trust our partner to catch us, and love is like a safety net below us. No matter what happens, we know that love will catch us, protect us, and let us have another chance.

We Want to Last

While some promote the idea that we should have multiple relationships throughout our lifetimes because we all change, I've yet to meet a couple who says "I do" who doesn't hope for that relationship to last their whole lives. We should seek to last just for lasting's sake. Two people can resign themselves to a bad relationship and endure until death. This isn't a goal worth pursuing. Instead, we want a relationship that lasts in such a way that in the end we can say it was all worth it. While bad times will come, we last to see better days. The lasting becomes another success that adds to the sweetness of our connection.

To laugh, love, and last—these are the desires of nearly every couple who walks down the aisle. They are reasonable desires that are far more attainable than some realize. But they don't happen in the way we expect. They are the byproducts of some surprising commitments.

The Lucky Ones

We use *lucky* to describe a successful marriage because we often can't see the skills and abilities required to make marriage work. We are a people focused on facades. We assume the outside of something fully defines the inside. We value the appearance of health more than health itself. When we see happy couples, we compare our marriage to theirs. We wrongly conclude they are happy because they have more money or a nicer home or a better-looking mate or a spouse who doesn't nag as much. We write simple conclusions to our complex problems and assume we are unhappy because we are unlucky. We think there isn't much we can do about it, so we long for something different while changing none of our own actions.

What if the lucky aren't so lucky? What if a successful marriage isn't about the forces of fate but the force of choice? What if we control far more of our relationship than we realize?

A good marriage looks like luck because there are few things on the outside that predict success in marriage. But inside a successful relationship, there are some hidden characteristics that lead to marital satisfaction. These are the secrets of the lucky ones:

1. They have right expectations of themselves and others. They don't overestimate their own ability. They know they are flawed and needy. They understand their partner is the same. In the midst of their mutual brokenness, they find meaning and value.

2. They confront the pain. They don't shy away from it or deny it. Instead, they grieve over the fact that they can't be everything they want to be. They name their imperfection and process through it.

3. They operate between apathy and aggression. They find the middle ground, avoiding passivity, which allows issues to grow, and evading aggression, which can blow something out of proportion. They are strong but vulnerable, realistic but not pessimistic.

4. They seek something higher than themselves. While their marriage brings a great deal of personal satisfaction, that isn't their ultimate goal. They pursue something bigger. This pursuit draws them out of themselves and into a greater purpose. It minimizes conflicts and accentuates commonalities.

5. They overflow with compassion. Empathy, understanding, and compassion are reciprocated between the two. They nourish their love for one another so that it impacts every aspect of their daily lives. They have a

genuine warmth for each other and do not allow their feelings to grow cold.

6. They create a wholeness as individuals and as a couple. They know who they are. They do not feel divided or torn by individual desires or what is best for them together. Truth is allowed to freely flow without being used to intentionally injure the other. They don't live in perfection, but they so consistently handle their mistakes properly that nothing is allowed to fester. Their integrity drives out any possible hypocrisy.

7. They are continually in the process of making peace. They understand their differences and strive to be united in their diversity. They welcome problems as an opportunity to learn more about each other and to grow closer together. They don't have more or less conflict than others, but they handle it in a more productive way.

8. They learn to take a punch. They understand their commitment to one another will not be understood by others, by a culture that easily attacks commitment. They know marriage can be difficult, but they believe the struggle is worth it. They use both external and internal challenges as a way to strengthen their bond.

These practices aren't readily seen. It's rarely possible to look at a couple and know if they truly have compassion for each other or if they are humble in their understanding of themselves and marriage. But these unseen qualities define a relationship—and create the kind of marriages we all want.

The map toward a better marriage is often unseen, but even if it's found, it's often ignored. The connected dots don't match our expectation of what would make marriage better. It's a contrarian's map. Not only are these eight principles not obvious, but they are quickly rejected by the masses when clearly stated. A few of the ideas aren't just ignored; they are fought against.

But if there was ever a time for contrarian advice when it comes to marriage, today is the day. Never have so many experts produced so much information regarding a topic with such little positive impact. Some have concluded marriage advice doesn't work, but is it possible that the conventional advice is simply wrong?

When the videographer comes to Aunt Elaine and Uncle Charlie's table at your wedding reception, they are well-intentioned when they look into the camera, confess their love for you, and give you the secret to marital success. Their intentions are good, but their advice is often bad. "Happy wife, happy life" might sound like solid marriage advice, but the cliché won't get a couple through the challenges of raising a child with Asperger's. While a husband should seek the well-being of his wife, the simplistic concept of "happy wife, happy life" is grossly dangerous. It implies a man is in control of a woman's happiness. It implies a woman's emotions are so fragile that they can destroy a marriage. It's conventional wisdom, but it's wrong. So is much of the clichéd advice given in wedding reception videos and in private text messages among friends.

Few people realize that "doing whatever makes you happy" probably won't actually make you happy. Discipline, far more than following desire, will lead to long-term satisfaction. "Follow your heart" sounds great in a tweet, but it is not helpful direction in a relationship that at times will test every aspect of your heart's resolve. "Love is all you need" sounds wonderful in a wedding card, but a lot of couples love each other even as they are divorcing because they can't figure out how to better communicate with each other.

The conventional wisdom has been tried and left wanting. These are the times for contrarian advice. A better marriage is found when you begin to practice the eight principles mentioned above, which contradict much of what you believe to be true about marriage. It all begins with the foundational principle that you have no idea what you're doing . . . and that's okay.

BE INTENTIONAL

1. Of the modern rules for marriage, which one are you most tempted to believe? What are the negative consequences of that belief?
2. When you think of the ideal marriage, who comes to mind? Why? What do they do that you want to emulate?
3. Why do we often believe happiness is more about happenstance than our choices?
4. What would a happy marriage look like to you?

HAPPILY HUMBLE YOURSELVES

It's like shooting them into outer space. With a simple pronouncement and a kiss—from him to her, not me to them—I introduce the couple as Mr. and Mrs. Whatever the Name Is That Afternoon and off they go. She's relieved all the wedding preparations have come to an end. He's excited the honeymoon is about to begin. They walk up the aisle with a relaxed confidence they did not have just an hour earlier. As they nearly sprint to their future, I want to hold them back and warn them of what lies ahead. They have no idea.

That cluelessness is probably a gift. If they knew every challenge that lay before them, they likely would not so easily proclaim their vows to God and man. Ignorance removes the hesitancy, and with a boldness akin to a four-year-old who believes putting on a Batman costume makes him Batman, a young couple innocently believes that putting on a white dress and tuxedo will make them an indivisible couple for the rest of their lives.

As they walk up the aisle and into the world, the dangers to their relationship are many.

They walk into a world that doesn't value marriage. Many believe it is an out-of-date covenant. Others believe it should be disposable. The very definition of marriage is no longer agreed upon.

They walk into a world full of temptation. It's always been present, but never has it been this accessible. Both husband and wife will hear many voices through the years daring them to forget their promises.

Time itself will be a great threat. Without intentional effort and energy, the couple's affection will wane. While their love at the wedding can feel overwhelming, they may soon struggle to feel anything.

As a couple walks away from me hand in hand, there is one threat that rises above all others—pride. Pride is marriage's only true enemy. Sure, there are other threats, but they all must be wedded with pride to have a negative influence. Show me a marital problem and I can show you pride at work.

Pride's by-products in marriage are diverse:

- Adultery is the prideful belief that I deserve something I'm not allowed.
- Contempt is the prideful concept that I am better than you.
- Silence is the prideful act that shows you don't deserve my voice.
- Anger is the prideful response that says I don't have to care about your feelings.

- The absence of sex stems from the prideful belief that I can ignore your needs.

At the heart of nearly every marriage problem is pride, yet rarely does a couple call me and say, "We have a pride problem." They might recognize the issue in their spouse, but they never see it in themselves.

Most of the time when we experience the absence of humility—pride—it comes in an unexpected way. Obviously there is the issue of arrogance. We all know arrogant people who think they have it all together and have no need of anyone else. Yet the truth is that most of us and most of the people we meet who lack humility are not arrogant; we are insecure.

Humility is like the lines painted on a road. It defines what is appropriate, keeping us out of the ditches or oncoming traffic. A humble person knows who they are. I would describe humility as a proper self-perspective when we compare ourselves to God. Knowing God defines our boundaries. When we know who God is and who we are, we can function within ourselves. The result is humility. When we're humble, we understand our limitations, don't have an inflated view of self, and don't try to control the world.

When we don't know our bounds, that is the result of an absence of humility. A lack of humility is the result of an improper self-perspective when we compare ourselves to others. When we take our eyes off God and turn them to others, we've lost humility.

When we compare ourselves to others and see ourselves as better than we actually are, the result is arrogance. When we compare ourselves to others and see ourselves as worse than we actually are, the result is insecurity. Both are the same problem—an improper self-perspective resulting in an absence of humility, expressed in completely different ways:

- An arrogant person won't need anyone; an insecure person will need everyone.
- An arrogant person will never consider that they might be wrong; an insecure person may never consider that they might be right.
- An arrogant person will never say "I'm sorry"; an insecure person will never be able to receive those words.

This two-sided coin of pride results in division. In the same way that humility unites, pride divides.

Show me a broken home and I'll show you one or two people full of pride. Show me a broken business partnership and I'll show you someone full of pride. Show me a splintered church and I'll show you the presence of pride.

How many bands didn't make it because the members worried about one person getting more songs or more fame than the rest? How many great teams won only one championship because the players were concerned about who got the ball the most? How many great churches fizzled and died because the leaders were concerned with who was making the decisions?

Pride divides and destroys. Humility unites and multiplies.

Built from the Ground Up

Here's some good news: pride dies in the soil of humility. The power of a humble spirit will ground individuals and a couple. When your relationship is planted in the soil of humility, it can thrive.

Humble is related to the word *humus*. Humus is the dark organic material often used in gardens. Decomposition has broken down elements to their lowest point, resulting in stability. Left to itself, humus will go unchanged forever. When added to soil, humus has many positive effects:

- It feeds the soil to make it more fertile.
- It allows for the coexistence of plants, animals, and microbes.
- It protects the good characteristics of other soils.
- It naturally extracts and destroys negative aspects of other soils.
- It retains water, allowing other soils to withstand droughts.
- Because of its porous nature, when other soils are too compacted, it allows for aeration.
- Its dark color helps warm the cool soil in spring and cool the hot soil in summer.

When added to other soils, humus brings life. It causes everything else to thrive.

What humus does for soil, humility does for marriage. When we are broken down to our most basic, stable form, unchanged by everything around us, we bring life. When we are humble, marriage is able to flourish. Humility:

- creates perspective so we can approach marriage properly
- allows for the coexistence of people
- brings forth the good in others
- naturally draws out and destroys the bad

- retains enough supply to get others through dry times
- is porous enough to bring air when others need a breath
- warms the cold and cools the warm

Humility rids a marriage of pride and allows two people to properly relate and grow. Because humility is beautiful, it's attractive. It naturally draws others to itself in a magnetic way. Maybe because it is so foreign to the human condition, humility intrigues us. This intrigue makes it sexy. A grounded person is attractive. They understand who they are and who they aren't. They aren't self-loathing, but they also aren't self-aggrandizing. They are so at peace with themselves that they focus more on others. They can be helped and uplifted by others, and they're not easily discouraged or brought down by outsiders. They are their own person even as they deeply care for whoever is near.

Humility leads to a proper confidence. It allows for growth and development. It gives a person the courage to explore while also being content with who they are. All of these characteristics are attractive. We are drawn to humble people. If pride is a marriage's ultimate threat, humility is a marriage's most important defense. When two people humbly love one another, they are drawn to each other while also maintaining their individual identities. Humility unites a couple.

Ten Warning Signs of Pride in Marriage

Few things are as toxic to a relationship as pride.

While no one denies the danger of pride in a relationship, it can be hard to identify its early warning signs. If we're unaware of its presence, pride grows in a relationship until it is nearly unstoppable. Let's learn to recognize the earliest appearance of it and do everything in our power to eradicate it.

Though this is not a comprehensive list, here are ten common signs of pride in marriage:

1. *Feeling everything is personal.* When pride enters us, everything becomes about us. Every opposing idea or differing viewpoint isn't seen as a natural disagreement or a difference of perspective; it's a personal attack on us. Our response to every situation is one of defensiveness because we feel assaulted even if our spouse simply disagrees over the most minor of issues. Pride prohibits us from looking beyond ourselves.

2. *Finding fault.* Because pride can require us to look better than others, a pride-filled person often becomes an expert at finding fault in others. It's as though we have fault-finding glasses, and once we view life through that lens, problems are all we see. Some of us seem to believe that finding fault is our gift, and we readily point out the faults of everyone—bosses, co-workers, friends, political leaders, referees, coaches, and even our spouse. When pride is present in a marriage, one spouse often sees the other as the source of all the problems. If her husband would simply change, everything would be okay. If he can replace this wife with a better woman, marriage would be easy. When we are so busy finding fault in others, we never consider what improvements we could make for the sake of the relationship.

3. *Refusal to be influenced by a spouse.* Humility opens us up to change, while pride paralyzes us in our current state. Whenever we are unable to be positively influenced by our spouse, it's a sign something is horribly wrong. It means respect has been lost—and the most common cause of lack of respect is pride. When we think we are better than our spouse, we stop being influenced by them.

4. *Ignorance of the needs of others.* Pride doesn't just keep us from caring for others; it prevents us from even seeing their need. Pride causes us to become so focused on self that we no longer see the hurts, struggles, and inabilities of our spouse. Not knowing their need, we cannot consider how we can assist with it. With our focus so fixed on what our spouse should be giving, we can't consider what we need to give to them.

5. *Addiction to attention.* Pride often demands attention. Believing ourselves to be of more importance, we assume everything is and should be about us. Everything becomes about what we want, think, and desire and how situations impact us. Even if our spouse tragically breaks their leg, we immediately think about how that will inconvenience us and not our spouse. Every issue is viewed through a self-centered lens.

6. *Refusal to submit to authority.* When we're prideful, we believe we have it all figured out, so we don't need to listen to an expert. Even if statistics show a certain action is negative, we'll assume we are the exception. In marriage, an arrogant person will not humble themselves to wise counsel or do what an expert says. But

when pride is present, help is never sought. Even if a prideful person attends counseling, they simply go so their point can be validated. This shuts them off from any potential help.

7. *Inability to see opposing viewpoints.* Pride causes us to crown our way of thinking as king. Anyone who sees the world differently is viewed as wrong. This may begin with outsiders to the marriage, but it will quickly include our spouse. If someone can't fathom another person voting a different way or having an opinion that differs, they are filled with pride. Yet life is complex. In marriage, few things are truly right or wrong. Most disagreements arise from different perspectives. But when pride is present, one spouse cannot fathom the other spouse having a different viewpoint. Any disagreement is a sign the spouse is wrong.

8. *Never asking for help, always expecting service.* It's an odd combination, but pride weds the two. When we overvalue ourselves, we refuse to ask others for help. We see it as a weakness. But at the same time we regularly expect others to serve us because we think we are due their sacrifice. So a man filled with pride will ask his wife for nothing but expect her to do everything. He will never consider how he can assist around the house or lighten her load. Instead, he will expect her to do it all while thanking her for nothing.

9. *Absence of sacrifice and submission.* Pride says we deserve to do our own thing and go our own way. Marriage demands that we sacrifice our individual dreams and desires for the sake of the relationship. It requires us

to submit our wills to one another in order for the union to flourish. Pride convinces us that sacrifice is below us and submission is unnecessary. While a healthy marriage is defined by both individuals submitting themselves for the well-being of the union, pride refuses to submit to anyone and does not sacrifice for anything.

10. *Refusal to say "I'm sorry."* The inability to apologize can appear for two reasons. First, if we're prideful, we may not be able to see we are wrong. Having never made a mistake, we see no need to apologize. Second, we might not be willing to admit fault even when we know it's there. While we might understand we have done wrong, we are terrified that an apology might show weakness, so we refuse to offer one. Either way, the words "I'm sorry" are never said, or if they are, they are quickly followed by "but you . . ."

When pride is present, intimacy is absent. A couple can be full of pride or they can have a healthy marriage, but not both. A wise couple will recognize the agony of pride and do everything in their power to eradicate it from themselves and their relationship.

The Goldilocks Principle of Marriage

Not too cold. Not too hot. But just right. In the children's fairy tale "The Three Bears," a little girl named Goldilocks enters an empty house owned by three bears—Papa Bear, Mama Bear, and Baby Bear. Each animal has a preference for the porridge. Goldilocks finds one too cold, one too hot, and one just right. The Goldilocks principle often references finding the middle ground of two extremes.

Within marriage, we need to find just the right perspective of how to think of ourselves—not too much and not too little. For a healthy marriage, we need to understand ourselves and our spouse in the proper way. When we think either too little or too much of ourselves, we will throw our marriage out of balance. We must think of ourselves just right.

Too Much

When we overestimate our value in marriage, we make marriage solely about us. Instead of understanding God's role in marriage, we assume marriage is simply about our feelings, satisfaction, and happiness.

When we think too highly of ourselves, a healthy marriage is not possible because our spouse can never be seen as our equal. We will always think that we deserve better and they are lucky to be married to us.

Too Little

When we think of ourselves too little in marriage, we do not give our full selves to God or our spouse. We withhold the fullness of who we are and in so doing dishonor God and cheat our spouse. This is often done under the appearance of humility. But it is a false humility. It's an undervaluing of who we are as beings created in God's image. It's thinking of ourselves less than who God made us to be. It's trusting our judgment over God's.

Thinking too little of ourselves can express itself in a variety of ways:

41

- being unwilling to communicate our true thoughts and emotions
- pretending to be something we are not
- expecting our spouse to read our mind
- assuming we deserve to be treated poorly
- excusing our spouse's poor behavior as our own fault
- exchanging genuine service for actions intended to earn the love of our spouse
- refusing to believe we deserve the love and respect of our spouse

While humility attracts, pseudo-humility repulses. Many people wrongly confuse humility with a poor self-esteem. They think if they aren't very confident, they must be humble. But insecurity is not humility; it's another form of pride. When we fixate on our weaknesses, inabilities, and mistakes, we are still focused on ourselves. Pride can express itself as thinking too highly of oneself, but it can also be seen in thinking too lowly of oneself. Humility is neither. A humble person has a proper understanding of who they are—refusing to overvalue or devalue themselves. More than anything, they simply don't think of themselves as much as a person filled with pride.

Pseudo-humility expressing itself in self-pity is not attractive. People might run to the initial cry for help, but before long they will be turned off by the self-loathing. A romantic partner might try to rescue someone with a pridefully low self-esteem, but eventually they will resent the partner for it.

When we think too little of ourselves, a healthy marriage is not possible because we will never fully engage in the relationship. Our spouse will always be relating to part of us and not all of us.

Just Right

Whenever we think of ourselves just right in marriage, we understand our proper place within the relationship. Knowing we were created in the image of God, we understand our value. By understanding we are the creation and not the Creator, we don't overvalue ourselves. This perspective breeds true humility.

A just-right perspective expresses itself as we:

- humbly communicate through both listening and sharing our true feelings
- feel a deep sense of gratitude for the opportunity to give and receive love
- show respect at all times and in a variety of ways
- continually learn how to be a better spouse and how to understand our spouse better
- deal with issues directly, but keep them in their proper context
- fully shoulder and share the responsibilities for making the marriage work
- appreciate where the relationship is but always strive to make it better

Seeing ourselves in the right context creates a climate in which a marriage can thrive. Both partners feel valued, grateful, and empowered to create a meaningful marriage.

Need over Image

If I could give every couple one gift as they walk up the aisle after getting married, it would be an insatiable desire to make their marriage work.

Recognizing pride and its dangers, I would instill within them a willingness to do whatever is necessary not just to have their marriage last for a lifetime but to create the best possible relationship they can have with one another. When will and desire are aligned, a couple can overcome nearly any obstacle.

One of the great gifts of humility is that it jettisons our concern about image. Most unhealthy couples are more concerned with appearing healthy than actually being healthy.

Just down the hallway from my office are the offices of two counselors. I regularly refer couples to those professionals. However, many people will refuse to see them. The idea of walking into a church office, past several of their pastors, and into a counselor's office is too much for them to bear. They can't stand the thought that others might see them going into a counselor's office. What would people think?

What those couples don't understand is what I think when I see people going into a counselor's office. While they may believe I'm judging them for having an inferior marriage, I'm actually doing just the opposite. I rarely know the actual issues that cause people to walk into our counselors' offices, but every time I see them do so, I think, *Good for them.* I'm grateful they understand their need for help. I'm happy they not only recognize their problems but are willing to do something about it.

The counselor I often use in my hometown has an office right on the main street. Someone once asked, "Do you ever wish you could park around back so no one would see you going in there?" I answered, "I'd be far more embarrassed if someone found me sneaking into counseling. I'd be ashamed if I ever gave the appearance that I was more concerned with my image than my need."

Humility causes us to care more about fixing what is wrong than appearing as though everything is all right. The Bible calls this being "poor in spirit." To me this brings up the image of a beggar. And even if it's uncomfortable, this image is important to hold on to. A beggar is driven to:

- humble themselves and ask for help
- show themselves incapable of solving their own problem
- admit they are helpless
- seek someone who can help
- try anything that might work

When this attitude is found in marriage, a couple is continually recognizing weaknesses, confessing sin, seeking reconciliation, learning new skills, being mentored by others, reading, studying, and doing everything in their power to move the marriage forward.

But when a couple cares more about image than need, all the forward momentum stops. They would rather allow a problem to continue than run the risk of someone finding out they are struggling. When they refuse to get help, their marriage languishes.

Recently a church youth group leader told me about the group's trip to the beach. Twenty teenage girls went, and they had a horrible time. Insecurity ran rampant and expressed itself in a thousand different fights. At any moment, any number of girls weren't talking to the other girls. They spent most of their time moping in the condo.

But for an hour each day, they put on their swimsuits, fixed their hair and makeup, went to the beach, and took selfies. The pictures were posted on social media, with #blessed or #grateful or #beachlife. Then the girls returned to the condo for another miserable twenty-three hours.

It's American teenage life in 2018. It's also the state of many marriages in 2018.

We live in a day in which the highest priority for many is to appear as though everything is going well. Forget reality. Deny the true condition. Simply dress up as best as you can so you can project the image you want others to believe.

It's hypocrisy. It's dangerous. And it's the way many people handle their marriages.

There are moments in which seemingly perfect couples suddenly appear anything but perfect. The marriage that looked so good on social media comes crumbling down in a dramatic way. Why?

In most cases it's because the appearance was a facade. Smoke and mirrors were being used in public ways to distract from the real issues going on inside the home. In most cases, the couple is intentionally putting on a ruse. In some cases, the couple, ignorant of what a good marriage looks like, has no idea their relationship is fake. Its ending is a shock to them.

Heart versus Facade

It's contrarian to this culture, but the focus of a couple must be on the heart of their relationship, not the appearance given to others. Our time, energy, and effort are best spent nourishing the inward reality of the relationship. Appearances matter, yes. We don't have to ignore what we project to others, but we don't want to fixate on it. If you find that you and your spouse speak kindly to one another in public, post loving pictures of one another on social media, and say all the right things when talking to others, but at home you're silent or short with each other, unkind and inconsiderate, and quick to serve everyone else but never each other, it's time to work as diligently on the heart of your marriage as you do on everything else.

The Heart of a Marriage

To work on the heart of a marriage, we put our energies in several areas.

The condition of our individual hearts. The heart of a marriage is most influenced by the spiritual condition of each individual heart. By protecting my own heart, I'm helping protect the heart of my marriage. By helping nourish the heart of my wife, I'm also nourishing the heart of our marriage.

Trust. A healthy marriage is a relationship defined by trust. Where trust is absent, disease sets in. Left unchecked, that sickness will destroy the whole relationship. Trust does not imply perfection, but it proves that even when mistakes are made, we know how our spouse will respond, having our best interests at heart.

Priorities. A healthy marriage is properly ordered. At minimum, the couple understands what they should and should not value. At maximum, they live every moment according to that value system. When a couple does not properly order their lives according to their values, disunity will arise. If they value time with one another but do not budget that time, there will be frustration. As a couple matures, they should become more skilled at living out their values. What they desire to do—honor one another, spend time together, learn and grow—they actually do.

Respect. The heart of a marriage cannot be healthy when disrespect is present. A couple does not have to like everything about each other, but they do need to have a deep respect for one another. When respect is absent, the heart of the relationship begins to decay.

Communication. How can a couple guard the heart of their marriage without learning to communicate with one another? A positive sign they are working on the heart of their marriage is when they prioritize communication within their relationship. Recognizing its importance and the struggle all people have to communicate properly, healthy couples continually seek ways to better communicate with their spouse.

Humility Empowers Growth

Where humility is present, so is growth. As pride divides a couple, it also impedes them. A litmus test of pride could be found in the question, "Are you growing?" The most likely reason a couple is not growing is because of pride. Either they are too proud to believe they need to grow, or they are so focused on the problems of each other that they aren't learning new skills, gaining more knowledge, or finding deeper levels of intimacy.

If a couple can grow, they can overcome anything. But when they lose their desire or ability to confront problems, find answers, and implement that knowledge, they are in serious trouble.

Marriage is not a static state. At every moment, each individual in the relationship is changing, the circumstances of life are changing, and what is necessary to be happily married is changing. Sadly, some individuals will boast about their own lack of growth. "She's changed," the husband says. "He's just not the same person," the wife says. They are often right in their description. The person they married is not the same person from five or ten years ago. But the problem is not that one spouse changed; the problem is that the other spouse did not.

Change is a necessary aspect of marriage. Unless you are growing and adapting, your marriage is dying. Healthy couples have the ability to learn and grow, and a humble couple soon learns:

- Their greatest teacher is often conflict. Any relational rub is an opportunity to learn a new skill, grow in knowledge of one another, reveal their hearts, and engineer a new element of the relationship.
- Success is not the same as satisfaction. While a healthy couple appreciates professional or personal success, they also have a deep awareness of the dangers of success. They work with great intention to find a deeper satisfaction with one another rather than allowing success to fill relationship voids.
- Failure is an opportunity. Healthy couples see failure as a tremendous chance to explore mistakes and make

better choices the next time. They do not blame one another but instead seek a mutual understanding.

This growth mindset does not come naturally. People are not born this way; they make choices to become this way. The first area in which they grow is in the area of weariness. They get tired of being tired, of repeating the same behaviors, of experiencing the same dissatisfaction.

Having grown weary of being weary, they make different choices, learn new skills, and develop in every aspect of who they are as individuals and as a couple. Begging for growth, they find it.

You Don't Have to Do It on Your Own

Humility knows something pride does not: achievements accomplished together are just as valuable as those accomplished alone. Whether you study alone or with a group, if you make an A on the test, it's an A. Whether you stop smoking cold turkey or do it via medical intervention, you still have stopped smoking. Whether the idea was solely yours or was the by-product of groupthink, your company still sells the product.

Pride tells us the great lie that something means more if we do it alone. If it is *my* idea, *my* accomplishment, *my* doing from start to finish, the outcome will be better. People will respect me more. The feeling of satisfaction will be deeper. Success will be sweeter.

But it's not. The outcome is the same, and sometimes the process is lonelier, tougher, and rife with more peril. Humility tells the truth: I don't have to do it on my own. Neither do you.

The things that are truly worth doing are worth doing no matter how they are done. Whether they're accomplished alone or together, what really matters is that they are accomplished. Humility knows we can almost always accomplish more together. It doesn't care who gets credit for the idea. It doesn't need recognition. It doesn't dissect every aspect to give proper due. Humility is more concerned with getting important things done than getting credit for having done something.

How many marriages stay adrift for decades because one of the spouses has too much pride to ask for help? How many careers never reach their potential because the employee feels pressure to go it alone? How many addicts continue to act out on their addiction because they won't admit to someone they need help? It's all pride. Humanity is not very good when left alone. We were created for community, for intimacy. We are complete as individuals but we thrive with others—with families, teams, communities, friends, and co-collaborators.

Pride warns us to stay by ourselves. It says we should go it alone to get all the glory and fend off any threats from others. Humility invites us to reveal our inabilities, admit our inadequacies, and seek help. What dreams are left unaccomplished? What addictions are still having their way? What projects are stagnant? What personal struggles keep repeating? Is it time to get help? Is it time to stop trying to do it all by yourself? Is it time to admit you can't figure it out?

Tell yourself the truth. You don't have to do it on your own. Any achievement accomplished with the help of others is just as valuable as one accomplished alone. And it could be that those accomplished together are sweeter because you have someone who knows the struggle it took to experience success.

> **PRACTICING THE COMMITMENT** One way to create humility is to find ways to serve others without them (or anyone) knowing. Together with your spouse, pick four people you would like to help. Each week for the next month, choose one of those people and help them. Do it discreetly. Find a way to ensure that they will not find out. Do not tell them or anyone else. Resist the temptation of posting something on social media or telling a friend. Discuss the action and aftermath only with your spouse. If the person asks you about it, don't lie—tell them you did it, but refuse to talk about it beyond that.

A Humble Anniversary

Nothing should humble an individual like vowing their earthly life solely to another person. Yet it's understandable why few couples walk down (or up) the aisle stripped of all relationship pride, knowing they desperately need help. Erotic love is such a powerful emotion that it can make a couple feel invincible. Many young couples can't even imagine the idea that they will fight, much less that they will have years of struggle and difficulty over a lifetime of marriage.

We know why young couples may have pride; what's confounding is how we still struggle with it a few months into marriage. Just a little bit of experience in marriage should quickly prove to every individual that they need help. While the wedding date may not be a source of humility, every anniversary that follows should give birth to a greater understanding of the dangers of pride and the fruit of humility.

Humility is unnatural. It's second nature for us to continually think of ourselves and to use others for our own desires. In part, the beauty of marriage is that when two people willfully choose to submit their individual well-being to the well-being of one another, love flourishes. But this is a commitment. It requires a continual trial and error, a process of failure and forgiveness, and a cognitive decision to develop humility. The decision can happen in an instant, but the process of being humble will take a lifetime. Yet no couple regrets traveling the road to humility.

BE INTENTIONAL

1. List several common problems in marriage. How could they be the result of pride?
2. Which of the ten common signs of pride in marriage are you most prone to? Why that one?
3. What does it mean to think of your marriage "just right"? Do you tend to think of your marriage too much or too little?
4. Why is humility a prerequisite to meaningful growth?

HAPPILY EMBRACE THE HURT

Some funerals are unforgettable. I didn't know the couple. They were enduring the most horrific days of their lives without much support. Through some mutual friends, I was contacted and walked with them through the trauma.

An otherwise normal pregnancy had taken a sudden, tragic turn. The excitement of labor had turned to the sorrow of loss. The day they should've taken their son home, they were in a funeral chapel. I had agreed to officiate at the service. I didn't expect a big crowd, but I was shocked by no crowd. No one showed up to support the couple. Had I known, I would have recruited friends and family to be present. But not knowing, I walked into an empty chapel, pulled three chairs around the tiny casket, and did the quietest funeral I've ever performed.

I doubt they heard a word I said. Who could blame them? As I sat and looked at the couple, their pain was overwhelming. Not only did I wonder if their marriage would last; I wondered if either of them would make it through the loss. Having opened themselves up to a love they had never felt before—the love of being a parent—they now experienced a sorrow that cannot be fully described.

It's not just cliché to say that love hurts. As someone who interacts with people every week during their darkest days, I've seen that the most common characteristic is that love is at the source of the pain. Without love, the most painful moments wouldn't be painful. Because of love, we experience pain and a grief we can't imagine.

Some feel the pain and write the wrong conclusion that to avoid future sorrow, they will simply never choose to love. They close their hearts to love, assuming it's the wisest thing to do. Sadly, this doesn't lessen their loss. We were created to love. Seeking to avoid pain by avoiding love simply leaves us with only the pain.

One of the guarantees of love is loss. As we open our hearts to love, we also open them to sorrow. One of the most memorable moments of my life was kneeling beside my grandfather to tell him that his wife of seventy years had died. The pain in his eyes is something I've never felt. I've sat in a living room and listened to a wife make groans I can't describe after she found out her husband was having an affair. I've wept with men as their hearts are breaking because their aging wives no longer recognize them.

Marriage hurts, though some of the pain is avoidable. We don't have to know what it's like to experience betrayal. Making wise financial choices could keep us from knowing the stress of financial strain. There are many ways we can avoid the pain and sorrows that are the regular experience of others. We can build trust, empathy, and gratitude so that our spouse feels supported and loved. Yet some pains can't be avoided. No matter what steps we take, we cannot fully insulate our hearts from sorrow. To say "I do" is not only vowing to love but agreeing to hurt. It's welcoming sorrow into our lives.

A healthy marriage requires a characteristic few consider. We cannot truly love well unless we mourn well. We live in a culture of denial. If we haven't recognized our poverty of spirit, we live based on image more than reality. To project the proper image, we must distance ourselves from pain, sorrow, and grief. To create the facade we desire, we must at minimum deceive others, but in most cases we deceive ourselves regarding how broken we actually are. Those who recognize their true nature and are more concerned with need for connection over image recognize and mourn the brokenness in themselves, others, and the world.

We Mourn Ourselves

The single life gives room for deception. When you are single, it's possible to think you are better than you actually are. Marriage removes the deceit. There is no question—you are highly flawed.

When you are single, when you get tired of people, you can find a way to be alone. Rarely are you seen at your most vulnerable. If you are wise, you can learn the times in which you should remove yourself from circumstances or situations that might tempt you to act in ungodly ways.

When you are married, you do not have the opportunity to escape, and the people in your life will actually force you into potentially sinful situations without you asking to be there. Nothing reveals the sinfulness of humanity like marriage and parenting.

Before I was married, I knew I was broken. But I had no idea the extent of my brokenness until I had a family of my own. The gift (and the curse) of a spouse is that you can't fake it with them. We can fake kindness, generosity, mercy, and forgiveness with others because we only have to do so for a set period of time. However, with my wife I could never fake those characteristics because I would have to do so for an indefinite amount of time. She is always there. I can't run to an empty room and hide—she will find me. I can't take a day off and say, "I'm not going to be your husband today." The role is 24/7 and she sees my true character. And often it is ugly.

But this is the gift of marriage: our true natures are revealed and we have the opportunity to genuinely change our hearts. The problem with faking life is that—we're faking life. We can deceive ourselves into thinking we aren't that bad. Marriage provides us the opportunity to change because it reveals to us our great need for change.

Consider just two aspects of our true nature that marriage reveals—selfishness and insecurity.

We want our way. Even the most laid-back, easygoing person desires to have things done their way. Marriage requires us to submit our desire to another, and submission rarely comes naturally. Even the most selfless person will have new revelations of selfishness once they are married. They might even discover that some of their seemingly selfless acts are motivated by selfish desires.

And we are needy people. We are broken, and because of our brokenness we attempt to protect our hearts. Yet marriage requires us to invest our hearts. We can't keep them hidden and be an effective spouse. No matter the aura we give at work or the reputation we have among others, we are all insecure people, and the intimacy of marriage reveals those insecurities.

Marriage is hard. While there are a variety of causes that make it hard, there is one unique characteristic that leads to the most stress. Marriage is difficult because it exposes your greatest wounds. Whatever those wounds may be—and we all have them—marriage will touch them. I guarantee it. Whatever the issue, marriage will expose that vulnerability:

- Your parents never complimented you as a child.
- You grew up feeling the weight of the world was on your shoulders.
- You have a fear of abandonment.
- You assume all men are evil.
- You think women are inferior.
- You were taught sex, even in marriage, is dirty.

This exposure will hurt. It will create doubt, fear, and uncertainty. It will cause you to blame your spouse or question the institution of marriage. It will tempt you to run from conflict, intimacy, and struggle.

The process of exposing our deepest wounds is painful, but it's also a great opportunity. While marriage isn't the only way to confront our greatest sorrows, it is one of the best ways. Within the context of a lifelong, committed relationship built on the foundation of love, we are given the opportunity to admit our greatest fears, confront our greatest failures, and work through our greatest struggles. In brokenness and imperfection, we can begin to reveal what we quickly hide in front of others.

Sadly, many couples never understand the opportunity before them. Instead of realizing that marriage will inevitably hurt, they assume the pain is a sign that something is wrong. Like someone working out for the first time and assuming the next day's soreness is a sign they shouldn't work out, many couples experience the natural soreness of growth within a relationship and mistake the pain as a sign the marriage isn't working. If they will simply continue to do the work, they could see great gains both individually and as a couple, but instead, they run from the pain and blame their spouse in the process.

Marriage is guaranteed to include pain, so we should do everything in our power not to add to that pain. Wise choices are essential so we don't suffer the unnecessary burden of betrayal, crushing debt, addiction, or many other sorrows that can happen by foolish choices. However, some of the pain of marriage can't be avoided. It needs to be accepted and appreciated. For many, the potential for marital success is determined by our willingness to endure pain, to mourn our own broken nature.

We Mourn Our Spouse

We mourn ourselves before mourning anyone or anything else. By recognizing our own bankruptcy first, it allows us to put the brokenness of others and this world into a proper context. Whenever we fixate on the failures of others without first considering our own failures, we become judgmental, unmerciful, and contemptuous. But when we mourn our brokenness, properly see our strengths and weaknesses, and are motivated to improve so that we minimize our failures as much as possible, we become a great spouse. We are empowered to see our spouse's struggles without allowing them to define the whole person. We have the ability to speak truth in love. We can deal with sorrow without becoming overwhelmed by it. We can stand for what is right while also being full of compassion.

Many struggle with loving others because they have not learned to love their true selves. Unable to confront the truth within themselves, repent, forgive, and move forward, they live in denial of their true natures and fixate on the flaws of others. This can be a source of great conflict in marriage.

Only when an individual confronts their own failings are they ready to deal with the brokenness of their spouse. And in every case, there is plenty to deal with.

My wife is great. She is kind, thoughtful, and smart. I can say of her what my grandfather said of my grandmother: "I'm not saying she is better than everyone else; I'm just saying there is no one better than her." It is one of life's greatest blessings that she married me. But she's not perfect. No matter how hard she tries, she can never fully be the woman I want her to be.

In many ways, this is good. She doesn't need to be everything I want her to be. Because of my selfishness and shortsightedness, I have many desires for her that are not healthy. It is a blessing that she is her own person rather than someone created in the image of my desires. If she was everything I wanted, we would not have a real relationship. Every opinion of hers would mimic mine. Every want would be the same as mine. She would simply exist for me. Clearly there is more to her life than that.

In other ways, the fact that my wife can never be everything I want her to be should cause us both to mourn. No matter how good she is, she's not perfect. In ways that frustrate me, her, and others, she is a sin-filled, imperfect person. Just as she and I have to mourn my own imperfections, we also have to mourn hers.

The difficulty in mourning is knowing what we should mourn and accept versus what we should mourn while demanding change. Some sources of pain should not be overlooked, while other aspects should be accepted as a normal aspect of being married to a fallen human being. There are specific failures that require change—abuse, repeated adultery, a refusal to take responsibility for the marriage, etc. But there is a difference between normal frustrations within marriage and relationship-threatening behaviors that can't be tolerated.

We Mourn Our Marriage

As I mourn my imperfection and the imperfection of my wife, it reminds me that our marriage will never be perfect. It is not immune to the fallenness of the world.

While marriage can lead to the betterment of both individuals, it perfects neither one. Couples wed when they are imperfect, and they remain imperfect throughout the marriage. Many of these imperfections come and go throughout the years. The early years of marriage should empower a couple toward maturity, removing some faults and flaws. Yet even as some areas are improved, new difficulties arise.

Some of your greatest sources of struggle in marriage aren't even known on your first, tenth, or thirtieth anniversary. As seasons change, new challenges arise.

The faster a couple learns to handle disagreements, the better off they will be. But some things never change. No matter how much effort, work, or attention a couple gives a specific problem, the underlying root issue will never change. The imperfection that was present on your first day as a couple will still be an issue on your last day. Marriage is never perfect.

Many issues cannot be resolved because there is neither right nor wrong. A couple experiences tension in an area because they have differing personalities, viewpoints, and past experiences. They simply see the world differently. These differences are a great strength in a healthy marriage but can wreak havoc in an unhealthy marriage.

Some issues will go unresolved because we are broken people. Try as we may, some of our faults cannot be overcome. We can learn to control them, compensate for them, and plan around them, but we cannot fix them. Deep wounds from our childhood or past relationships will play a part in our current relationships. Someone from a broken home might always struggle with trust. A spouse who grew up with an alcoholic parent may never be able to fully relax at a party where alcohol is served. If an individual suffered a major trauma, fear may always influence their relationships.

But just because an issue cannot be resolved does not excuse the couple from working on it together, from accepting each other's failings. A husband and wife may have to continually discuss a situation, renegotiate a common ground, and determine the best course of action. While the amount of work does not diminish, the expectations from each spouse can be changed. On some issues they aren't expecting to forever settle the dispute. They are simply seeking to find a common ground to help them through today, this year, or this season. This change in perspective doesn't make the process easy, but it does lessen the burden on the couple.

Knowing "some things will never change" is not a mantra to allow a spouse to repeatedly cheat or continually engage in a destructive behavior. Some flaws must change for a marriage to survive. If a behavior is damaging the family in significant ways, it must be confronted. But not all actions fall into that category. An active addiction cannot continue, but a repeated frustration because your spouse isn't as expressive or family minded or thoughtful as you desire may not change.

Since some things will not change, here are four ways to respond to each other in our brokenness:

1. Determine what is acceptable and what is not. This is not an easy practice, but we must determine if something is an acceptable flaw or it if falls into the category of something we cannot tolerate.

2. Draw clear boundaries on the things that must change. If something is not acceptable, we must communicate our boundaries very clearly. For example, I would not live with an active addict. That's a boundary. It gives my spouse a choice of how to deal with her addiction, but it does not hand over control of my life to her. She has her choices; I have my own.

3. Negotiate a common ground on things that can't change. On most issues, couples can deal with them

but it will take a lot of negotiation. If one spouse likes to be on time but the other doesn't mind being late, the couple must discuss their feelings. They can make plans to lessen the stress on each other. Ultimately, each spouse must consider the feelings of the other regarding the issue.

4. Mourn the areas you wish were different. It's healthy to grieve the imperfection. Recognize it, admit it, grieve it, but then appreciate the good aspects of the relationship. By mourning what we wish was different, we will better be prepared to appreciate what is good.

In marriage, some things never change and that is okay. As long as we can find a way to manage life in the midst of what we wish were different, our relationships can still thrive despite the weaknesses.

We Mourn Our Culture

The difficulty of marriage begins in our own hearts, is complicated within our marriage, and is also deeply impacted because of our culture. We live in a society of shattered relationships. The brokenness is so much, we can't overestimate it. In response to a culture of broken marriages, we must mourn. We feel sorrow over the loss. We hurt for people who go through divorce. We weep for the parents and the children. With the same gravity as we treat death, we should treat divorce. It's that tragic.

We mourn for many reasons, but one specific benefit comes from doing so—we don't judge what we mourn. Judgment is born from a lack of empathy and compassion. Whenever we don't feel for those who hurt, we judge them. We assume ourselves to be better than them. We separate ourselves from them, believing we could never do what they have done. We overestimate ourselves and underestimate them. When mercy is present, we mourn. But when mercy is absent, judgment flows.

The irony is that what we judge, we become. I'm not sure why it happens, but it is a clear pattern. Those who judge the harshest most often fall for the same sin they judge. It's possible their judgment is a sign they are already involved in the sin and are trying to direct attention away from themselves. Or it could be that their arrogance, which leads to judgment, is the same arrogance that prevents them from doing the work necessary to protect themselves. Either way, they become what they judge.

Brokenness is all around us. Our culture overflows with marriages that are broken or breaking. Our only appropriate response is mourning. Doing so gives us empathy for those hurting and humility within our own marriage.

PRACTICING THE COMMITMENT   Lament is a literary device in which someone voices their disappointments but reaffirms their love. Write a lament concerning your marriage. Put into words ways in which your marriage is not everything you want it to be. Do not excuse bad behavior, but do recognize the imperfections of yourself, your spouse, and your marriage. Maybe illness has limited your travel, or aspects of your spouse's personality aren't exactly what you desire. List ways you know you aren't everything your spouse would want, but end with words of appreciation for what you do have. Recount why you love your spouse, what you appreciate about marriage, and what you look forward to in the days to come.

Mourning Motivates Action and Appreciation

Grieving our imperfections and the sorrows of life has a distinct purpose: to motivate us to action. As we are moved to act, our heart is filled with a deep appreciation for our spouse and life.

There is a subtle difference between productive mourning and a process that could hurt a relationship. One type of mourning heals, while the other kills. Some will recognize the failures within their relationship and will further injure the relationship. Others will see the same faults, but the awareness of their imperfections will lead to a better marriage. The difference is in what mourning causes us to do.

Unproductive mourning leads to apathy. Some wrongly conclude that since we can't be perfect (or our spouse can't), we should stop trying to be. Often out of fear, they refuse to learn, grow, and improve. Instead, they give up, blame, and whine.

Productive mourning leads to action. Seeing our failures in marriage empowers us to do better. Even as we know we can't be perfect, we see the opportunity to improve. Because we know we will fail in some areas, we work hard to succeed in the areas we fully control. When we do fail, we attempt to learn from it so we do not repeat our mistakes.

Strangely, stepping out of denial and into the truth of our failures can lead to a deep sense of appreciation in marriage. My wife is keenly aware of my flaws. There are times I feel sorry for her for being married to me. Her adventurous, outgoing spirit has to be frustrated by my cautious, homebody nature. Yet her awareness of my flaws does not bias her against me. She is able to see my weaknesses but still love my strengths.

Recently I had one of those long days, in every way. Most days aren't that way, but this day had been crazy. It began early, ended late, and was packed for every second in between. As an introvert, I was exhausted. I love people, but I need time by myself to rejuvenate.

Jenny knows this. Although she had worked all day, including the last two hours with kids in the house, she knew what I needed, knew my weaknesses. She took the kids, left the house, and gave me an hour to decompress. I felt many things in response to this, but the most prevailing emotion was appreciation, the by-product and benefit of healthy mourning.

We all face the temptation of apathy. It's often bred by proximity. After experiencing something for a long period of time, we can lose sight of the good we have. As time passes, we lose appreciation for the most important people around us. No marriage is exempt from seasons in which one spouse fails to communicate appreciation for the other. Life gets busy, we become focused on our own tasks, and we fail to recognize the contribution our spouse is making toward our lives. It's expected to happen in seasons, but it's inexcusable for it to be an ongoing characteristic of marriage.

Appreciation is a vital aspect of marital satisfaction. This might be an oversimplification, but many times we are satisfied to the extent that we feel appreciated. While appreciation is often a by-product of a healthy marriage, it also helps create the healthiness. Because the human tendency is to grow accustomed to things we see on a regular basis, we must diligently cultivate a culture of appreciation within our marriage. This will occur as we see the good in the midst of, not in denial of, the bad. Even as we recognize each other's flaws, we also see strengths.

Appreciation must be:

- *Felt.* It's not enough to know our spouse is adding to our life. We have to feel it. We wrongly assume we don't control our feelings, but they're under our control much more than we realize. We can feel appreciation as we take the time to focus on what our spouse is doing, understand their contribution, and recognize how our lives are bettered by them.
- *Expressed.* Once appreciation is felt, it needs to be expressed. We must find meaningful ways to communicate our gratitude to our spouse—in the most likely ways our spouse will hear it. One of the best questions we can ask is, "What are three instances in which you felt appreciated by me?" The answers will give us insight into how our spouse best receives expressions of appreciation.
- *Reciprocated.* While feeling and expressing appreciation is important, it's not fully experienced until it is reciprocated. Feeling gratitude for what our spouse does for us should motivate us to work harder in serving them. In the best of scenarios, both spouses experience a repeated cycle of feeling, expressing, and reciprocating appreciation for one another. This creates a positive

momentum in which each spouse feels appreciated and challenged to show appreciation for the other.

The presence of appreciation can have dramatic effects on a marriage. When we appreciate someone, we treat them differently. We empathize with them, forgive them, listen to them, enjoy their company, give them grace, and serve them.

Failure is not exclusive to unhealthy couples. Because every married person fails, every marriage will experience failure, even healthy relationships. Many shortcomings will be insignificant in nature. Others may threaten the foundation of the relationship. The difference between marital bliss and marital destruction is not simply the absence or presence of failure. It's the difference between how those failures are perceived and handled.

While failure is present in every relationship, don't downplay its effects. When we do not live up to the vows we made to our spouse, those choices have negative consequences. We can't minimize or deny them. We can't just brush them off because they are a part of life.

Yes, we are all imperfect, but our imperfections hurt others. Those hurts matter. They must be recognized, admitted, and properly handled. If they are not, we will heap sorrow upon the sorrow our spouse already feels.

Just because failure is universal does not mean we can ignore it. But we can try to avoid it. It is far easier to stay out of trouble than to get out of trouble. Wise choices before we make a mistake far outweigh wise choices after a bad decision. Because we are destined to fail, we should work hard to prevent failure. We can't just throw up our hands and do nothing.

We must understand that we can't completely eliminate failure from our lives or the lives of others. We will fail our spouse. Our spouse will fail us. At times our marriage will be disappointing. But mourning, not rejection, is the proper response to that disappointment.

BE INTENTIONAL

1. Why is action a result of proper mourning, while apathy results from denial?
2. What are some ways in which you can't be everything your spouse needs in marriage?
3. Describe some aspects of marriage that aren't what you expected.
4. How does mourning increase appreciation in marriage?

HAPPILY AVOID BOTH APATHY AND AGGRESSION

The back-to-back meetings could not have been more striking. I was uncomfortable within the first thirty seconds of meeting with Aaron and Amy. They entered my office angry, and each one became more upset with every word that was said. Everything was an attack. To my knowledge an affair had not occurred. They weren't drowning in debt. No major outside event had threatened their marriage. They were on the brink of divorce, and it looked as though they were going to go out with a bang.

I couldn't even figure out what the main issue was. Neither could stay on topic. One issue would lead to another, which would lead to another. They were interrupting each other, talking over each other, and continually accusing each other. Aaron and Amy were the poster children of what we typically think of when it comes to a couple on the verge of divorce. I could tangibly feel their disgust with each other.

By the time they left my office, I was exhausted. When Beth and Steven entered, my ears didn't have the capacity to handle much more yelling. And they wouldn't have to. The couple was silent. Every question I asked was answered with one word or a shrug of the shoulders. Neither was willing to start the conversation. I had to drag every thought out of both of them. It was nearly impossible to understand what brought them to my office because no one was willing to say what was wrong. They were unhappy, but they couldn't tell me why. They wanted more but were unwilling to reveal what they needed more of. Rather than hating each other, Beth and Steven seemed to feel nothing for each other or for themselves.

These two couples, who on the outside couldn't have looked more different, were suffering internally from the same problem: neither were able to deal with the issues between them. Unable to constructively discuss minor frustrations, major disagreements, or anything that put them at odds, they were headed for divorce. They were simply going to get there in different fashions. Aaron and Amy were going to explode, while Beth and Steven were going to decay.

When I think of marriage, it reminds me of driving. My grandfather taught me how to drive. While my parents had moments of instruction, the bulk of the effort went to my grandfather. It was a wise approach—grandparents tend to be more patient than parents, and children tend to take instruction better from someone they don't live with on a daily basis. At my first lesson, my grandfather told me driving was pretty easy—make the truck go at a reasonable speed between the two lines. It's a simple approach—drift too far to the right and you're in the ditch, drift too far to the left and you're in the path of oncoming traffic. Keep it in the middle and you'll be just fine.

In marriage, dealing with conflict is very similar. Every marriage is certain to experience conflict. Opinions will differ. Expectations will diverge. Small disagreements will occur. Major conflicts will arise. There is no way to avoid conflict in marriage. And we shouldn't want to.

Conflict provides our greatest opportunity for transformation. Without it, we likely wouldn't change, grow, or mature. A healthy marriage requires a good amount of conflict. But few people enjoy conflict, so whether consciously or unconsciously, we naturally attempt to avoid it. What we need to do is keep it between the lines.

Meekness is the method needed to keep marriage between the lines. It keeps us out of the ditch and out of the path of oncoming traffic. It allows us to keep moving forward without crashing. The absence of meekness leads to the ditch of apathy or the oncoming traffic of aggression.

For over two decades, I've officiated at wedding ceremonies. Hundreds of couples have spoken with me about marriage and then stood before me in order to get married. Yet I've never been asked, "How should I act in marriage?" Not once. When I go to a new restaurant, I research what I should wear and what the atmosphere is like so I will know how to act. I take great effort to teach my children how to act in different situations—to be quiet in a library, loud at a basketball game, and still during a movie. There is an expected way to act in various circumstances. Meekness is how we should act in marriage.

A healthy couple navigates everyday life meekly, neither apathetically nor aggressively. They bridle their power in order to steer the marriage in the most profitable direction. Meekness combines gentleness with strength, submission with initiative, humility with ability. Marriage at its best is meek.

When someone acts in a meek manner, they quickly act on behalf of another but are never self-serving; reject passivity and take action, but only for the good of others; and are neither weak nor overbearing. This is the method of marriage. Not weak. Not a limp noodle or a broken spirit, but a person fully alive, active, and engaged. Not a tyrant, a hothead, or a self-centered jerk, but a person restrained by love and grace.

Meekness is not:

- avoiding an issue
- demanding your own way
- being afraid to rock the boat
- trying to win the fight

It is:

- engaging the important issues
- finding a workable solution
- courageously revealing your heart
- trying to win the relationship

A marriage thrives when we live out our vows with meekness. Issues are confronted with just the right amount of passion and grace. We are quick to speak on important issues and slow to do so on trivial issues. Our strength is always used to protect the ones we love, never to exploit them.

Confronting Aggression and Apathy

If meekness is the effective operating system of a healthy marriage, aggression and apathy are the viruses that can shut down the relationship.

Aggression and apathy must be an aspect of every marriage. The problem is not their existence but their improper application. Meekness is knowing when to be aggressive and when to be apathetic. The problem with humanity is that we rarely get it right.

Aggression can be good. If choosing sports teams, I want an aggressive point guard or an aggressive defensive tackle. If picking coaches, I want an aggressive coach who tries to win instead of trying not to lose. If buying stock, I want a company with an aggressive CEO. If my daughter isn't being treated right, I want her to have an aggressive defender. However, when not properly determined or directed, aggression can be destructive.

Humanity was created strong. We had gifts and a calling. In the Garden of Eden, God gave us a task—to show dominion over the earth. Our power was to be used for bringing glory to God and good to the earth. Our strength was for assisting in his creation and asserting his will. But we didn't use aggression for God's glory. We used it for rebellion. We stepped beyond the boundaries he had set.

At the same time, apathy isn't always bad. There are many things that don't deserve our attention or effort. Just as we were created to be aggressive, we were also created with the ability to restrain that aggression. We were given the skill to scan our horizon and understand what deserves an increased awareness and what can be ignored as meaningless to our existence.

Consider the beginning of humanity. Eve assertively went beyond where she was allowed to go and ate the fruit of deception. Adam passively watched his wife, refusing to use his God-given strength to stop her.

This story is a microcosm of our lives—we're aggressive when we should be passive, passive when we should be aggressive. Both actions share a common theme—rebellion against the command of God. When we take our God-given gifts and apply them in the wrong places or fail to use them in the right places, chaos ensues.

And a chaotic world is where we live. We have no reason to believe that others will use their strength for us, and we have every reason to believe that others will use their strength against us. Some respond to this world in an aggressive manner, believing "I've got to get them before they get me." Others respond to the chaos in an apathetic way, believing "No matter what I do, I can't win." Neither is a good approach to life—or marriage.

When aggression and apathy are wrongly applied in marriage, insecurity becomes the defining characteristic. Trust is lost, and a person does not have the security of knowing their spouse will respond in the right way to important issues. They may even have a certainty that their spouse will *not* react properly—whether by blowing trivial issues out of proportion or showing no sense of passion to the things that really matter.

The unseen irony is that aggression (anger) and apathy are two sides of the same coin. While they express themselves in radically different ways, they are both defense mechanisms to protect a hurting heart. The husband who yells at his wife when times are tense has the same motive as the husband who refuses to look away from the game when his wife is trying to reveal her heart. Both are attempting to avoid an intimate conversation that might demand transparency and honesty from them. Both are trying to shut down their spouse, but they are using different methods. In the same way, the wife who attacks her husband at every instance, and the wife who says "Nothing" when asked if something is wrong even though something is obviously wrong, are both avoiding a real relationship even though their approaches are radically different.

This is what misused aggression and apathy have in common—avoidance. Both are schemes in which we attempt to check out of the hard aspects of being in a relationship. When we are afraid of what might be demanded from us—revealing our thoughts or feelings, experiencing pain or vulnerability—we choose actions that avoid difficult experiences. In most cases, we don't recognize what we are doing. It's not a conscious choice to shut out our partner and protect our heart. It's an unconscious response to fear, in which we naturally embrace behavior that was modeled for us while growing up or that we have found productive in adulthood. Of course, this behavior isn't productive to the relationship; it is only useful in avoiding the immediate source of our fear.

To act in a meek way demands that we don't run. We stay. We have the courage to risk our heart, be vulnerable, show transparency, and figure things out. No matter the situation, we must stay engaged in the relationship. This is why when our spouse is telling us something, we listen. It's not about the content of the conversation, it's about the relationship.

When your husband is telling you about a play in the game, it's not about the game but about his heart. When your wife is recounting what happened in her day, it's not about her day but about her heart.

In this regard, marriage is like the military. When someone enlists, one of the goals of training is to make it second nature for them to engage. Even in situations where the average person would run the other way, the one wearing the uniform must subconsciously engage the situation. So it is with a healthy marriage. Through years of training and trial and error, a husband and wife must train themselves to engage in the relationship. Avoiding issues—through either silence or violence—damages the marriage. Engaging in a meek manner honors their spouse, values their marriage, and empowers success.

Meekness Keeps a Small Fight Small

The difference between healthy marriages and unhealthy marriages is not the volume of conflict but the intensity of each encounter. Two couples can squabble over the same issue. The first couple experiences the disagreement and confronts the issue, and within a short period of time it's as though the conflict never occurred. The second couple can face the same tension, but that frustration explodes in intensity, and years later one spouse can still remember the painful fight.

Why can the same issue be a minor blip on the radar of one couple and be a major explosion within the relationship for another couple? The difference is meekness. In healthy relationships, meekness cushions the strain in the midst of tense moments.

It's interesting that as divorce has increased over the last half century, the word *meekness* has disappeared from our vocabulary. It's a symbolic illustration of what is wrong with marriage. As meekness becomes foreign to us, conflict becomes common.

Tension is certain to arise within a relationship. Disagreements arise. Conflicting opinions are held. Wrongs are done. Conflict within a relationship cannot (and should not) be avoided. Yet it must be handled properly. While no one fights perfectly, healthy couples handle conflict in a restrained way. They fight within boundaries. They communicate with guardrails. They become more thoughtful when the tensions rise. They use restraint to:

- stay on topic
- refuse to make the issue personal
- choose words wisely
- seek to solve the issue rather than win the argument
- work to understand as much as to be understood
- admit mistakes
- apologize
- overtly communicate love and affection

Restraint is an example of meekness. Meekness is not weakness. Pride has such an elevated standing in our culture that we often assume meekness is a negative quality. We confuse it with being weak, but meekness implies strength. Restraint assumes strength. It is power under control. It is strength that humbly submits itself.

Whenever a healthy couple experiences conflict, their frustration doesn't trump their wedding vows. They promised to love one another, and even in the midst of disagreement, they continue to love. They submit their desire to be right on an issue to the greater purpose of being in the right with one another. This doesn't mean they avoid a topic. If anything, meekness actually causes a couple to have more tension because meekness cannot remain quiet when a problem arises. It doesn't allow someone to be passive-aggressive or manipulative.

Meekness causes a spouse to speak, but it greatly influences how they speak. They may sometimes have a sharp tongue, but in the moment their tongue is restrained. They may have the wit to win any argument, but they restrict their minds from being used improperly. They may have information that could hurt their spouse, but they view that information as off-limits.

Love restrains us. It keeps us from using our strength as a disservice to our spouse. Our strength is best used for the benefit of our spouse, not for their detriment. Meekness keeps our strength under control.

Unhealthy couples aren't meek. Whenever an argument arises, they do whatever it takes to win. A continual game of one-upmanship is played as each spouse tries to injure the other even more. A wife's tone is improper, so her husband speaks louder. As he begins to yell, her words become more personal. As she attacks him, he becomes angrier. His anger enrages her. Both partners negatively feed off one another as the tension rises.

What began as a tension about a specific issue quickly grows into a fight over a variety of topics. Multiple issues are brought up as every past hurt or mistake is used as a weapon to injure the other. It's not unusual for a fight to grow to such an extent that the couple forgets what caused the original disagreement. All they know is how bad they each hurt and how much they desire for their spouse to feel the same pain.

With unhealthy couples, neither spouse ever lessens the tension. Every action escalates the emotions. Because of this, little fights become major. Small disagreements threaten the relationship. And fighting becomes unbearable. For this reason, some couples stop fighting. They can't take it. Issues are ignored. Words go unspoken. Hearts are hidden. It's understandable but unfortunate.

Other couples continue to fight. Each disagreement runs the risk of being the last, but they don't know how to stop. Every scenario has the potential to cause a major explosion.

Meanwhile, healthy couples experience the same conflict about similar issues, but they gently navigate them without any lasting negative impact on their relationship.

Cultivating meekness means we learn the skills necessary to stay under control, to fight wisely, and to love even when we disagree. If the tension rises, we step out of the specific issue and reiterate the big picture—how much we love one another. If our tone is wrong, we recognize the danger and soften our words. If another issue is brought up, we acknowledge that it's a discussion for another time, then come back to the original topic that began the conflict. If a personal attack is made, we call it "out of bounds" and remind each other what is acceptable and unacceptable in the midst of disagreement. If we are unable to fight as we should, we take a time-out but always come back and finish the conversation.

When we fight in a restrained way, the argument always stays within its proper context. A small fight stays small. A little disagreement doesn't hurt the relationship.

If small fights often become big fights in your relationship, consider the following questions:

1. Do you move from the topic at hand to some other issue—often a past conflict?
2. Do you attack one another rather than the issue?
3. Do you try to win the argument at all costs?
4. Do you say whatever comes to mind rather than restraining your words?
5. Do you retaliate when you feel your spouse has hurt you?
6. Do you threaten actions like divorce or violence?
7. Do you belittle your partner and disrespect them?
8. Do you talk at your spouse more than you listen to them?
9. Do you blame your spouse and refuse to take any personal responsibility for the situation?
10. Do you storm in and out of conversations without explanation?

If you answered yes to any of these, it shows an absence of meekness.

The Pressure of Disagreement

As a child, it was an unmistakable sound. The rhythmic noise of steam escaping through the little valve meant Mom was cooking with the pressure cooker. Water was put in a sealed container along with whatever the meal was for the evening. At first nothing would really happen. But slowly the heat began to rise. As it rose, so did the pressure. The "jiggler" would begin its dance. Pretty soon, supper was ready.

When disagreements in marriage go wrong, they mimic a pressure cooker. Everything causes the heat to rise. As it rises, so does the pressure. Before long, the communication becomes destructive. Some experience the negativity of disagreements and wrongly conclude they should do everything in their power to avoid them. They don't voice opinions, they steer clear of soft spots, and they stuff any frustrations internally rather than dealing with them externally.

While we don't have to confront every issue, we must learn to handle disagreements in an open, honest, and productive way. The answer is not to avoid disagreement. It is to reduce the pressure while we discuss the disagreement.

If couples can minimize the pressure they feel during a disagreement, they will be free to handle differences in a useful way. They will hear and be heard. They will influence and be influenced by their partner. They will grow and learn about themselves and one another.

Pressure can be prevented in several ways:

- Start slow. Few things determine how a tough conversation will go as much as how it starts. Begin with the wrong tone or attitude and the conversation will immediately be sabotaged.

- Stay on topic. Many times pressure builds as a couple moves away from the issue at hand and brings up old arguments. This is why it's important to settle issues—so they won't be brought up again. Forgiveness and resolution can prevent a couple from having recurring fights. Beyond resolving issues, simply having the discipline to stay on topic can prevent pressure.

- Discuss issues, not people. In unhealthy relationships, every problem is a person. Instead of seeing the issue as something outside the couple, they each view it as a problem with the other person. Instead of debating people, healthy couples debate issues. Problems are things they face and attack together. They are outside of the couple. When marriage goes bad, the problem becomes the spouse.

How to Release Pressure

No matter how much care we take in preventing pressure from building, on occasions it will rise. It's unavoidable. But when that happens, there are some simple steps couples can take to calm the tension and get back on track.

- Lower your volume. As pressure builds, voices rise. While some believe it's just their personality to yell, they are wrong. Refuse to yell at your spouse. By lowering your volume, it calms your own emotions and expresses calmness to your spouse.

- Soften your tone. It's not just volume that counts. Someone can have a quiet but sharp tone that attacks their partner. Do not speak to your spouse like they are a child, but do take great care in speaking softly and kindly.

- Voice the big picture. When pressure rises, put the problem in context. Remind your partner of your love, your shared desires, and the fact that this is just one issue. Step out of the conversation, remember the big picture, then step back into the disagreement. By doing so, you will put the issue in context.

- Take a break. Sometimes couples need to take a break from the conversation. But this only works if you truly come back and finish the discussion. If emotions are running high, verbalize your inability to have a good conversation at this moment, take a break, and then return to the issue. The person who calls for the break should give an exact time in which they will return to the conversation. Taking ten minutes, an hour, or a day can ease pressure.

I never did like anything cooked in the pressure cooker. The sound was never a good sign for me. But all these years later, I often think about that jiggler. When a discussion begins to turn tense, I try to imagine how hard the jiggler would be shaking. Keep things calm and a disagreement can be useful. Let the pressure build and the conversation is sure to be cooked.

PRACTICING THE COMMITMENT Recount an old disagreement in which you displayed either apathy or aggression. You may have displayed apathy by withholding your true feelings or saying things were okay when they weren't. You may have displayed aggression through a raised voice, sharp tone, or hurtful words. Replay the argument in a productive way. What would have been a wise way to handle it, in which you were fully engaged but not enraged? Talk about how the discussion should have happened and dissect why you think it got off course. How could the conversation have been saved after the first mistake or two?

Identify your negative habits during tense times. Give your partner permission to kindly point out the moment you begin to drift toward those habits. Use the word *happily* as a reminder that you need to choose better than to drift toward apathy or aggression.

How to Make Your Spouse Feel Heard

When couples avoid aggression and apathy, the result is that both spouses feel heard, understood, and appreciated.

"He/she just doesn't listen to me" is one of the most common complaints I hear. Even if they wouldn't define the relationship as unhappy, when pressed, many spouses feel unheard.

While no relationship is perfect, good relationships are characterized by good communication, which, in part, demands that we recognize we are bad at communicating. Some couples are deceived into thinking that individually they are capable communicators—those are the couples who never communicate well. Good communication begins with a recognition of the difficulty of the process. Yet healthy couples learn, grow, and develop proper communication. Meekness empowers the growth. The result is that both spouses feel heard.

Notice it's a feeling. It's not enough for a husband just to hear his wife. She has to *feel* as though she has been heard. While a husband is not ultimately responsible for his wife's feelings, he is responsible for doing everything in his power to give her the opportunity to have that feeling of being heard. She owes him the same.

Of course, the feeling had better imitate the action. When some men ask, "How do I make her feel heard?" what they are actually asking is, "How do I make her feel heard without actually listening to her?" They want the good results without any of the work. If your wife feels heard but you aren't actually hearing her, you will eventually be found out.

The goal is not only to hear our spouse but to have them believe they are being heard at such a deep level that they feel it. Not only do their heads believe it, but their hearts can sense that we truly listen to what they say.

We fail to listen for several reasons:

1. *Bias.* Our opinions color everything we hear. We are predisposed to listen to things we agree with and to ignore ideas we disagree with. Because men and women are inherently different, we are often biased to ignore our spouse. Instead of seeing their perspective as a valuable alternative to our own, we simply ignore it.

2. *Fear.* We often don't listen to our spouse because we are afraid. Whether that's because they might say something hurtful or they might say something we know is true, fear keeps us from listening.

3. *Contempt.* Some of us don't listen because we can never imagine our spouse having something worth saying. Believing we're smarter, more moral, or just better than our spouse, we never listen to what they have to say.

4. *Focusing on our turn.* The number one reason we fail to listen to our spouse (and others) is our preoccupation with determining what we will say. Notice this in your next tense discussion. We tend to focus far more

on what we will say next than on what the other person is saying. This prevents us from hearing our spouse.

Meekness prevents all four of these issues and empowers us to listen well. In part, creating a climate in which a spouse feels heard is as simple as learning some basic communication techniques. No one is born a good listener. We must develop the skills—through learning and practice—to become good listeners.

Here are five basic steps to good listening:

1. Stop talking. It's that simple. You can't listen while talking. Your spouse needs a chance to speak.

2. Stop preparing your response. Respond after your spouse finishes talking. Focus on what they are saying, not what you will say next.

3. Desire to know your spouse's opinion. Just wanting to hear what they have to say aids listening.

4. Listen with your ears and your body. If your eyes are on the TV or your phone, you aren't fully listening. Eye contact, facial expressions, and an engaged mind are key to listening.

5. Ask if you heard correctly. Before responding, clarify what your spouse has said. "Are you saying . . . ?" is a great question. Until they agree that they're saying what you think they're saying, you aren't ready to respond.

Listening well is loving well. We listen to those we love. Consider a grandfather working hard to understand a grandchild's broken sentence. Watch a high school student talking to his crush on the phone for the first time. Think about two lovers reunited after a long absence. In each case, love creates active listening.

When most people think about a bad marriage, they imagine a volcano. Every interaction is volatile. The house is full of yelling, insults, and flying objects. Most people think a marriage goes bad with a bang. In some cases that's true, but far more often marriages don't end with a bang . . . they end in silence. While aggression expressed in anger is a real threat to marriage, a greater threat might be apathy. More couples simply drift apart rather than repulsing one another. In either case, an absence of meekness is the problem.

In a healthy marriage, couples are aggressive in important issues and passive in things that don't matter. They will passionately fight for their marriage, for their spouse, and for the truth. They will be fully engaged in the relationship. But they will be laid-back about differing expectations or backgrounds. They will laugh at tensions that cause other couples to fight. They take seriously what others overlook and overlook what others take seriously. Their secret is a meek approach to their relationship. They take their God-given strengths and use them for the benefit of one another. They take comfort in trusting that their spouse will be there for them but won't overreact to issues.

Every week couples come into my office to talk about problems. In each case I see one of three responses. Some are trying to protect their heart through anger. Having been hurt so much, they aren't willing to be hurt again. Others are trying to protect their heart through apathy. Having tried and failed, they are no longer willing to put out any effort. Still others are fully engaged. They aren't perfect. They don't know everything they should do. But they are humble, teachable, and ready to get to work. When both spouses are part of the last group, their marriage has a tremendous chance of success no matter what problems they face.

BE INTENTIONAL

1. When are you tempted toward aggression and when are you tempted toward apathy? Which is more prevalent in your marriage?

2. Consider the ten questions on page 84. Which one least describes you and which one most describes you?

3. When pressure or tension rises in your marriage, how does it express itself in you? In your relationship?

4. Why is listening such a key ingredient to avoiding both aggression and apathy?

COMMITMENT 4

HAPPILY SEE MARRIAGE
AS BIGGER THAN YOU

When the Rolling Stones first released their single "Satisfaction," the song was so controversial in Britain that it only played on pirated stations. Fifty years later, the controversy is gone and "Satisfaction" is often viewed as one of the greatest songs of all time. The song's popularity has much to do with its simple title and memorable guitar riffs, but more than anything it speaks to the human desire for contentment.

We all want satisfaction. Mick Jagger's refrain of not being able to find it is a story many can relate to, especially in marriage. Jagger is right in assuming that a sexual experience can bring some sense of satisfaction. He's not the only one who tries and tries to find meaning between the sheets. If satisfaction can be found anywhere, we would assume sex is the place it would most likely be discovered. Despite our assumptions, human history has long found that even a great sexual encounter can't bring lasting satisfaction.

Simply put, sex does not satisfy. It was never meant to. A false assumption is that a sexual encounter will bring lasting satisfaction. It can give us a glimpse to such meaning, but sex itself was never meant to be the source of satisfaction. Lasting meaning, contentment, and value are found when our marriage is about more than just us.

We often believe satisfaction is a by-product of having our hopes, dreams, and desires fulfilled. So we make our relationship more and more about us. Yet the more we do, the more frustrations grow and restlessness is experienced. It's not until we look outside of ourselves that we can begin to experience what we are looking for.

Dehydrated Marriages

Thirst is a built-in mechanism of the human body through which the brain signals a need for fluid. Most of who we are is fluid, so thirst is a warning that we are losing ourselves. If we don't act on our thirst, we will die. Yet all of us at some point or another have probably failed to act quickly enough on our thirst. We have gotten overheated and dehydrated.

Dehydration follows a process. First lethargy sets in. As our fluid level decreases, our body tries to protect us by making us unmotivated to work. Our energy plummets and we don't want to do anything.

If those signs go untreated, dehydration can begin to affect our vision. Our peripheral vision blurs and eventually we get tunnel vision before we lose our sight.

If completely left untreated, dehydration will result in delirium. We will begin seeing things that aren't there, not seeing things that are, and living in a completely altered state of reality.

Lethargy, changed vision, and delirium are signs of dehydration. These are also characteristics of marriages that aren't nourished.

Most couples begin with tremendous passion. When dating and in the early years of marriage, couples work hard to see, communicate with, and understand one another. Nothing can stand in their way of being together. But energy fades as the demands of life and lack of intention starve the relationship of its needs. Slowly apathy grows.

Just as in dehydration, an undernourished marriage loses its peripheral vision—the people and interests outside our door. We begin to lose the proper focus of other things. We overvalue their condition and influence. We begin to look at others in a better light than they're actually in. We then compare that best possible view of others with the worst view of our spouse and marriage. We feel like we are missing out. Tunnel vision sets in as we pick apart everything that's wrong in our relationship, unable to see what's good.

Eventually delirium sets in. We begin living in a false reality. Reason is thrown out the window, and we live by our own ideas. Long-held standards that we would never violate are discarded. We strip our spouse of their humanity, perfectly willing to ignore them or degrade them. We loosen moral boundaries and are tempted to make poor choices that could destroy the relationship. We diminish the value of marriage, the importance of our vows, and the consequences of allowing a marriage to degrade.

We live in a society of dehydrated marriages. Everyone sees the symptoms, but few people understand the cure. Even worse, many people attribute a cure to the wrong source. They believe everything would change if:

- their spouse would get better
- their wife was sexier
- their husband was in better shape
- they had married someone different
- they had more money

While being in shape and having a few more dollars might not hurt, neither of those will hydrate a marriage. We need something far more.

Marriage Must Be Bigger Than You

The cure for a dehydrated marriage doesn't lie inside the marriage. It rests beyond it. Satisfaction is found when we realize marriage is bigger than us.

At our worst, each of us views marriage as "all about me." My spouse exists to satisfy my needs. Marriage is about my happiness. As long as I feel content, I will live out my vows. But the moment my spouse no longer makes me happy, I am free to take back my promises and do as I please.

We are better when we view marriage as less about us and more about others. Instead of thinking it's all about me, I understand marriage is also about my spouse. I'm concerned with her feelings, well-being, and happiness. It's also about the kids, extended family, and community. I look at my vows as influencing more than just me.

At its best, marriage is bigger than just each spouse and even bigger than the family. Marriage was designed to be bigger than us. That doesn't diminish us. It doesn't mean we aren't important. It doesn't mean we should never think about ourselves. But it does mean our happiness, satisfaction, and desires do not reign supreme in our marriage. The marriage we're hoping for, the one that stays strong, must be bigger than us.

Apart from God, this isn't the case. Through a secular mindset, marriage is simply about the individuals involved. It's a tool whose primary focus is personal fulfillment and desire. If you find a marriage that makes you happy, stay there. If you don't like the current arrangement, forget your vows and do as you please. Without God, marriage is about you.

A Christian perspective doesn't deny the importance of personal happiness or the role that marriage can play in satisfying desires. However, those ideas are secondary to a higher purpose.

Declaration of Intent

This design for marriage is modeled in a wedding ceremony. It's an aspect overlooked by many brides and grooms, but traditional wedding ceremonies have an intentional design. They often begin with the giving of the bride. This tradition is a holdover from a darker time when women were seen as property, but it can continue with a purer purpose. It's a reminder to the groom that the bride is a gift. She is loved by God and her family. They are willing to give their cherished daughter to the groom under one condition—that he loves her the way they do. The bride is expected to see the groom in the same light—as a gift she is called to love with the same passion as his mom and dad love him. What immediately follows is called the declaration of intent. It's what most call the "I dos."

Most people assume they are saying "I do" to each other, but they aren't. The declaration of intent is made to God. It often follows a question such as, "In the presence of God and these gathered friends, do you choose _____ to be your husband/wife?" When the individual says "I do," they have declared to God their choice. They are answering the question from God's representative in the service—the pastor or priest. After telling God of their decision, a couple then declares their commitment to one another. ("I promise to love you, to listen to you, to learn from you," etc.) This design is intentional, and it reminds us that before it's about us, marriage is about God. While we make promises to each other, our first promise is to him.

When Marriage Is Bigger Than Us

In its proper context, marriage is bigger than us. It is a tool God uses to shape culture, grow communities, and transform the hearts of individuals. In nearly every mention of marriage in the New Testament, it is a discussion that takes place in the context of the local church. That's why divorce doesn't hurt just the individual or family; it threatens the well-being of the church as well.

When a couple embraces the bigger picture of marriage, each aspect of the relationship is viewed through a different lens. Instead of someone thinking only of how a situation impacts them, everything is seen in relationship to the individual, the couple, the family, the community, and God.

Because of the importance of marriage, knowing the relationship isn't all about us creates a sense of urgency for some topics. If marriage was just about me, I could ignore problems or deny issues I don't want to face. Since marriage is bigger than me, I don't have those options. I must communicate problems. As a couple, we must face issues and improve our skills. Others depend on us loving one another well, so we must learn to do just that.

Because marriage is bigger than us, other issues become less important. Small irritations or frustrations are viewed through a different lens. They are seen as one problem in the midst of much larger contexts. If marriage is all about individual happiness, there is no issue too small to ruin the relationship. Yet if marriage is about the individuals as well as the whole community, some issues might be worth discussion but are not worth risking the well-being of others because of a personal preference.

Without a right perspective of marriage, we lose the right context to understand individual circumstances. We downplay important problems while elevating minor frustrations. We live out of balance.

However, whenever we understand the place of marriage within our lives, we have the ability to view each circumstance within its proper context. We can evaluate each situation with the right understanding of whether it can be ignored, laughed at, or seen as a simple irritation, or whether it's something we must take very seriously in confronting.

When We Are Bigger Than Marriage

Individuals who elevate themselves above marriage do so at the peril of the relationship and themselves. Clearly the relationship suffers. If either spouse sees himself or herself as the centerpiece of marriage, the relationship will be out of balance. Its success will fall to the whims of individual desire, which can change at any moment.

Yet what is often lost in this paradigm is the damage this view does to the individual. We might think that when we elevate ourselves, we will experience more fun, happiness, and excitement. It might not be fair to others, but at least we will get what we want. However, self-centeredness never delivers what it promises. Even as we seek our own desires, we do not find them.

A self-centered spouse is not happier, more content, or more joyful than someone who puts marriage in its proper context. When we elevate ourselves above marriage, we end up diminishing both ourselves and marriage.

A Higher Pursuit

Just as a gas engine can't run off of a different form of fuel, so too a marriage cannot experience health when it is attempted outside of its intended design. While individual happiness, desires, and considerations are important within a marriage, they are not the central focus. More than anything, marriage is an avenue through which a couple can know God and express him to others. Secondary to that pursuit are the desires of each individual.

When we pursue God through our marriage, we can experience the full potential marriage has to offer. When we simply focus on ourselves as the central figures of a relationship, we will know neither God nor each other.

A Bigger Marriage Endures

When we believe marriage is bigger than us, it empowers us to endure difficult times. It not only gives endurance; it produces a purpose for the difficulty. It's no wonder that as marriage has become more about us, lifelong commitment has diminished. If marriage is primarily about your happiness, your satisfaction, your well-being, and your contentment, a time will quickly come in which you aren't happy, satisfied, well, or content. In those moments, what keeps you married? Even if you stay married, what motivates you to do something about the state of your marriage?

Marriage is about the transformation of our hearts to be more like God. This is our pursuit. Happiness, satisfaction, emotional well-being, and contentment are all by-products of a healthy marriage. These are secondary results, not the main pursuit. The primary focus of a marriage is to become more like God.

It's our desire for God, more than our desire for our spouse, that can keep us married in the tough times. Marriage is about a joint pursuit of the heart of God. And few things can assist us in experiencing the character of God as much as marriage.

Marriage reveals our brokenness. Marriage and parenting are the two avenues in which God most often reveals my broken heart. I never knew the depths of my selfishness, pettiness, or crankiness until I got married. I've always known I needed to change, but marriage revealed how much change is needed. It also has shown me my desperate need for grace. I don't need just a little forgiveness; I need a level of forgiveness I could never earn.

Marriage reveals our brokenness in the safety of covenant love. Marriage reveals the depth of our depravity, but it does so in the safest of environments. It is only after we say, "I do, forever," that we truly begin to see who we have married. If the revelations came before the promises, the promises might never be made. While I'm tempted to hide every fault and flaw, the safety found in a committed relationship allows me to reveal my sinfulness, knowing I won't be rejected by my spouse. We expect each other to discover sinful mindsets and behaviors. Instead of hiding them, we expose them in order to let God transform those areas of our lives. Without the security of covenant love, it would be impossible to have the courage of revealing who I really am.

Marriage provides accountability to change. Because we are both pursuing righteousness, marriage gives me the freedom to reveal my true nature, but it does not provide the liberty for me to continue in my sinfulness. If I don't change, my wife knows it. If I'm continuing in a behavior, she has the right and the responsibility to call me on it. Transformation rarely happens alone. Marriage provides an automatic accountability partner as we spur each other on to good works.

I've been a pastor for over a decade, and during that time I've seen a lot of couples go through difficult times. There is a common characteristic among the marriages that make it—through the difficulties, both people are willing to work on themselves and the marriage. When one quits or will only focus on the other person changing, the marriage fails. Yet when both are open to work and change, the marriage normally makes it.

When we see marriage as an avenue in which God is transforming our hearts to be like his, we will view all challenges in marriage as opportunities to learn about ourselves, about God, and about what changes we need to make to become more like him. We will see them as opportunities to receive God's grace and to give that grace to others.

Considering Your Marriage

Ask the average couple, "How's your marriage?" and they will pause. Some will eventually give a pat answer of "It's good," while others will struggle with a response. But the pause is telling—few people know how to even process the question.

Ask a coach, "How's your team?" and they know how to answer. Ask your co-worker, "How are sales?" and they know how to answer. Ask a friend, "How's your golf game?" and they know how to answer. Ask a teacher, "How's your class?" and they know how to answer. But ask someone, "How's your marriage?" and they will fumble and stumble. Why? Because most people never look at marriage as something that can be improved. From the very beginning, they take a passive approach to their relationship, failing to understand its true nature. They treat it as though it's out of their control. They pretend like marriage just happens.

A coach sees a team as unique. A teacher looks at a class as individuals but also as having a collective identity. Businesspeople often view their business like another family member. We view teams, classes, and businesses as individual entities, but we often fail to view marriage that way. We view it as impacting our finances, affecting our lives, and defining our parenting, but we do not understand our marriage as having its own identity. We rarely consider and evaluate it in isolation.

Few things have the potential to increase marital satisfaction as viewing marriage as its own entity and then prioritizing that entity properly. A poor perspective of this has several negative consequences:

- It puts personal responsibility at a distance.
- It leads to passivity in the relationship.
- It makes problems feel unsolvable.
- It raises the amount of blame between the couple.
- It increases the sense of helplessness for both individuals.
- It blurs boundary lines, especially in parenting.

All of this occurs because a couple fails to see marriage for what it actually is. There is a reason marriage is often called an institution. It is an entity created for a purpose. It stands alone. It's one of the few things in my life that is so important I wear an outward sign for all to see that I am aligned with another person.

When we recognize our marriage as having its own identity, that empowers us to take charge of it. We can create the relationship we desire—we can evaluate it, change it, improve it, and make it become what we want. Until we view marriage in this way, we are destined to drift—and drifting rarely leads to the outcome we desire.

After we see marriage as its own entity, we then must prioritize that entity properly. Having recognized the true nature of marriage, prioritize the relationship in a way that will produce the result you want. While marriage is not the most important thing in life, there are few things of more importance. Once we identify our relationship as its own thing, we can place it in the right order in our lives. For me, it's second—just above my children and right below my personal relationship with God.

By failing to recognize marriage as its own entity, couples cannot prioritize it properly. Everything ends up coming before marriage because the couple can't see it for what it is. When marriage continually takes a back seat, it's likely the couple has failed to view it properly.

When marriage becomes a top priority in our lives, we invest in it. Threats are identified and neutralized. Problems are confronted. Effort is extended. Skills are learned. When marriage is important, we do what is necessary to make it succeed. But we can't make it important until we see it as having its own identity.

PRACTICING THE COMMITMENT Marriage is designed to be bigger than us. Together with your spouse, pick one couple whose marriage you admire. Describe why you admire them. What attributes do they display? How has their relationship impacted you?

Now list what positive impact you both could have on others. If you were happily married for the rest of your days, what would be the impact? How could you help others? What would be the legacy among your kids and grandkids? And what would happen if your marriage wasn't a positive experience? How would others suffer if you divorced? What would be the negative impact on your family, friends, and community?

A Desire That Drives

I have a friend who is an amazing musician. When people want to record, he is the first they call to play guitar. When someone has an event with music, his band is the main draw. Every Sunday he's one of the first in the church building, volunteering his time by playing music. It's not unusual after church or after a gig for people to come up to my friend and say, "Man, I wish I could play the guitar like that." If he doesn't know them, he smiles and thanks them. But if he knows them well enough to be truthful and funny, he says, "No you don't. If you really did, you would go home and practice. If you really wanted it, years ago while in school you wouldn't have gone to the party on Saturday night; you would've stayed home and practiced your guitar like I did. If you truly desired to play the guitar well, you would have sacrificed hours upon hours to perfect the skill. It's nice to say, but you don't *really* want to play guitar like this because it takes far more time than you are willing to give."

Making our marriage about more than just us is not only a mental desire that pops into our head on occasion. It is a desire that drives action. It's a hope that motivates and influences everything we do. It's a perspective from which everything is viewed.

This begins individually. I can't make my spouse desire something beyond herself, and I have very little time to try. I must focus on my own attitudes, decisions, and actions.

It continues corporately if my spouse joins me in the belief that marriage is bigger than the two of us. If she chooses not to believe that, then I continue to live out my vows and trust that God will use our relationship to transform my heart.

If she joins me in that perspective, then I thank God for her mindset and we work together to pursue righteousness.

We start with the heart. As we each focus on our own hearts, we also guard the heart of our marriage. We learn to love what God loves. We purge our hearts of desires that do not match his. We recognize our responsibility to have a heart for one another and the things of God. We are quick to act if our hearts begin to falter. We invest in our hearts, knowing they are moldable and can have their affections influenced.

We continue with the mind. We understand there are many lies we tell ourselves and each other. We attempt to learn the truth and live the truth. We hold one another accountable and speak honestly into each other's lives. We lean on the wisdom and experience of others to mentor and train us. We take what we have learned and attempt to help others.

We focus on our souls. We recognize there is more to life than what we see. We know our marriage is under attack from both outside forces and internal temptations. We seek to nourish our souls in worship, prayer, and gratitude. We create a community of like-minded people who can love and support us even as we love and support them.

We use our strengths. We exert ourselves for the betterment of each other and others. We engage in activities and habits that will build us as individuals, strengthen our marriage, and contribute to the well-being of society. We don't grow weary in well doing, believing there is a higher purpose and reward for doing the right things.

We have a deep concern for our neighbors. We believe God has allowed us to love one another in part for the benefit of others. We believe our relationship will diminish our weaknesses and multiply our strengths so we can better serve others. We believe God has placed us in a specific place and time for a specific purpose. We serve, expecting nothing in return from those we serve but expecting much from the process of serving. We believe that giving to others will strengthen our bond with each other, help us keep our lives in proper perspective, and greatly benefit the community.

We do these things because we hunger and thirst for righteousness, but we never expect these things to give us righteousness. We know that right standing before God and each other is a gift we cannot give to ourselves. But in response to what we have been given, we strive to do right.

Satisfaction is a universal desire. In a world of discontent, we all long for a deep sense of peace. The most common way we hear of to experience true satisfaction is through material things—more money, fame, or sex. But Jesus shows a contrarian way. Pointing us in a direction we would never believe could bring satisfaction, he says that hungering and thirsting for righteousness will lead to what everyone else is trying to find.

I've often wondered what it must be like for a former wife or girlfriend of Mick Jagger to listen to the song "Satisfaction." It must make them feel as though they have failed. They could not give Jagger what he desperately desired, so he continued to look elsewhere. Sadly, it's not a foreign experience for most spouses. Societal expectation is often that sex—and only sex—can satisfy. When it doesn't, people are left looking elsewhere. Mercifully for the women, the song is not a loud announcement of their failings. They were never designed to give a man lasting satisfaction. The song is a symptom of Jagger's wrong understanding of where satisfaction can be found. Every time he went to a woman seeking it, he missed an opportunity to share with her a satisfaction he could have found in God.

When we seek from our spouse what can only be found in God, we are setting them and ourselves up for failure. We will ensure our relationships are never as satisfying as they can be because we will always be expecting more. But when we have a proper perspective of what marriage can and cannot do, we empower success. We free our spouse from the pressure of making us happy. We free ourselves from disappointment when someone else fails to make us happy. No longer caught in a trap of wrong expectations, we can do what we are called to do. We can love and be loved, fail and succeed, learn and grow. Ironically, as we stop seeking satisfaction from marriage, we often find marriage much more satisfying.

BE INTENTIONAL

1. In what ways are you lethargic regarding your relationship? How has your vision blurred? Is there any way you are delirious regarding your marriage?

2. What's one purpose of your marriage that is bigger than you and your spouse?

3. How does seeing marriage as bigger than you make your marriage better?

4. How would you describe the current state of your relationship—dehydrated, thirsty, hydrated, or overflowing? Why?

COMMITMENT 5

HAPPILY REFUSE POWER STRUGGLES

An employee is consistently late to work. You let it go for some time, but finally you have the talk. You explain the value of hard work, the importance of everyone playing by the same rules, and your expectation that he be on time. He promises to do better and you're happy to have the problem solved.

The next day, he walks in right on time (actually three minutes late, but close enough), and you are thrilled with the progress. But on day two he's late. He couldn't even obey for two days. You can feel your blood pressure rising. You are tempted to storm into his office and fire him. You feel disrespected, lied to, and taken advantage of. In all your years of work, you've never been late without letting your boss know what was going on. Yet this employee continually abuses your kindness.

It's time to cut him loose. But before you do, you might want to ask him one more question. After telling him everything you've seen, what you think is happening, how you feel, and what you are about to do, ask, "Is there anything I'm missing? Help me understand how I'm wrong." In most cases the employee won't have much to say. He might even want to be fired. But every now and then, he will break. Maybe a parent has cancer. Maybe his marriage is in trouble. Maybe he has financial problems and his car is not reliable. In those moments, you will go from wanting to fire him to wanting to help him. Your resentment toward him will become empathy. With one piece of information, everything changes.

In their book *Crucial Conversations*, authors Kerry Patterson, Joseph Grenny, Ron McMillan, and Al Switzler describe the "Path to Action" that people take. First, we tie every action to an emotion. We feel, then we act. Feelings obviously come from things that happen—what we see and hear. But according to *Crucial Conversations*, the Path to Action isn't that we see/hear, then feel, then act. There is another step. After we take in information, we interpret before we feel and act. It's the interpretation that determines our feelings and then our actions.[1]

Our brains have a tremendous ability to take partial information and fill in the rest of the story. At no point do we ever have all the information. This makes interpretation a necessary part of life. We read people's body language and interpret their opinions. We see the letters that have been selected and interpret what can complete the puzzle on *Wheel of Fortune*. We watch an employee walk in late day after day and we interpret why.

In many cases we are right. Except when we aren't. On occasion, we see what is happening but write a totally wrong story. We think the employee doesn't care when in reality they have cancer. We think they are disrespecting us when actually they are trying their hardest to take care of a sick parent while still doing their job.

We are right a lot, but sometimes we are wrong. Knowing that we can be wrong should give us pause.

When Jenny calls me, I normally answer. Unless I'm in a meeting and simply can't, I pick up the phone even if I'm busy. Imagine if Jenny called one day at lunch and I didn't answer. She wouldn't think much about it. The day would continue without her giving it a second thought. Later that night after I get home Jenny decides to do some laundry. I change clothes and bring her my pants from the day. Knowing me, she checks the pockets before putting them in the wash, and she pulls out a receipt for a local hotel, stamped that day at noon.

In that moment, you would rightly assume that having remembered the phone call and seen the receipt, Jenny would be very upset. She would feel betrayed, angry, and confused. Those feelings could cause several actions—yelling, crying, and possibly murder. But I know Jenny. She wouldn't feel any of those. Instead, she would feel pride, empathy, and compassion. Her actions might include offering to fix me dinner or trying to give me some time apart from the kids to decompress. Why would her feelings and actions be so different from what most people would expect of her?

It's because her interpretation would be different. She would assume the best. She knows me. She knows the decisions I make. She knows what is most likely to happen in my day. In the scenario given, the most likely explanation would be that I was helping someone at lunch, which is why

I didn't answer her call, and that I got them a hotel room, which is why the receipt was in my pocket. Maybe it was a woman in an abuse situation who needed out of her home. Maybe it was someone who had a fire and needed a place to stay. Whatever the circumstance, Jenny knows it would make more sense that I did something good rather than assuming I had an affair.

Yet Jenny is also smart. She wouldn't just turn her head to something that could be serious. So she would likely bring the receipt to me and calmly ask, "I found this receipt—what is it for?" If my answer satisfied her, the issue would be over. If it didn't, she might have some more questions.

When two interpretations can be given for the same piece of information, healthy couples don't duck their heads to all negative information. Yet they assume the best and then verify their interpretation. This is the gift of good intent, and it's a gift of mercy.

At the heart of a loving marriage is mercy. All relationships require an element of mercy to succeed, but no relationship needs the continual flow of mercy as much as marriage. In the healthiest marriages, mercy oozes in every nook and cranny of the relationship. There is no place in which kindness and grace are not at work.

Being able to give and receive mercy naturally flows from the previous principles. If a person recognizes their need and grieves the imperfection of marriage, they are more likely to act in a meek manner. When they see their marriage as being more than just about themselves, they can give mercy even as they receive it.

But the call to mercy is a frightening one. It is fraught with risk. We are paranoid people in a paranoid world. And with good reason. There are plenty of people who would quickly abuse mercy within marriage. They will take and take and take, but the moment their spouse needs mercy they will refuse to give it. In part, this is why we must be careful who we marry. Because marriage will reveal the totality of who we are—every broken piece—we want to be cautious about who we welcome into our lives. Marry the wrong person and a continual flow of mercy may not be an option.

However, most spouses would do well to risk mercy. It never comes naturally. It always takes courage. Every couple will have times when one spouse gives mercy and the other does not. But if they stick with it—they keep trying and learn from mistakes—a couple can know how to give and receive mercy.

Marriage Needs Mercy

There are plenty of marriages that exist without mercy. Records of wrongs are kept. Revenge is exacted. A continual power struggle seesaws, depending on who has the upper hand at the moment. Characteristics of merciless marriages are regularly evident in cold shoulders, sulking, bringing up past mistakes in current arguments, joking about your spouse's weaknesses, turning disagreements into personal attacks, blaming your spouse for every problem, refusing to be influenced by your spouse's opinions, and assuming you are better than your spouse.

When marriage is attempted without mercy, it's full of skepticism, doubt, and uncertainty. Both individuals know that one mistake gives their spouse the upper hand. The marriage is defined by a continual power struggle.

Marriage with Mercy

A marriage defined by mercy is radically different. Outsiders may not notice, but those on the inside will see an obvious difference. When both spouses choose to show mercy to one another, they create space and freedom. Letting mercy flow between them allows both individuals to relax—to recognize they will make mistakes, but to know those mistakes will not be used against them or held against them.

When mercy is present, my actions are not dictated by my spouse's choices. I will treat my wife in a loving and kind way, no matter what she does. I will give her a grace she does not deserve. And she will reciprocate.

My wife needs me to be merciful to her. And I need her mercy because:

- There are times I willfully do what I don't want to do.
- There are times I unintentionally choose things that will hurt her.
- There are qualities or characteristics she desires in a husband that I do not have.
- We are both prone to miscommunication and misunderstanding the actions of one another.

What Mercy Is Not

While mercy might express itself in a variety of ways, it's important not to misunderstand what it is.

Mercy is not denial. Ignoring problems within the relationship is not an act of mercy. Denial is born of fear and cowardice, not love. Couples who refuse to confront problems are failing to love one another and themselves properly.

Mercy is not excusing poor behavior. Seeing a problem but excusing consistently bad behavior is not mercy.

Mercy is not becoming a doormat. Mercy is an act of strength. It isn't allowing another person to do whatever they want to do to us. It doesn't mean we continually suffer because of the poor choices of others.

What Mercy Is

Mercy is an action. It's not a feeling. Saying "my wife was merciful" does not simply define how she felt; it defines how she acted. It's the by-product of feeling love, compassion, empathy, and grace. It's the kindness of a spouse to patiently endure the negative consequences of my faults while assisting me in making improvements. It's the self-control of a spouse not to return evil for evil but instead to love even when it's undeserved. It's the humility of a spouse to understand that while our weaknesses express themselves differently, they are the same.

A good marriage can't exist without mercy. In the best of scenarios, marriage is defined by two people continually giving and receiving mercy. I need many things from my wife, but what I need most is mercy.

Avoiding Power Struggles in Marriage

Mercy is the antidote to one of the great problems within marriage—power struggles. Relationships often struggle because we desire to control each other, sometimes out of fear because we've been controlled in the past, sometimes because we don't trust our spouse to make wise decisions.

Many times we had this control modeled for us growing up, where one parent ruled over the other. Whatever the source, power struggles are destructive to relationships. We can either control or love our spouse, but we can't do both. Our vow is to love, not to control.

Mercy is the answer. Power struggles are built on the idea of inequality, and mercy levels the playing field. In a balanced relationship, though one spouse may take the lead in some aspects and the other spouse takes the lead in other areas, in every way they feel equal. When a relationship becomes unbalanced, one or both spouses are attempting to hijack control. They stop interacting with one another on an equal plane. Everything is used to get the upper hand on the other spouse—intelligence, morality, money:

- "I'm smarter than you, so I'm in control."
- "You are immoral, so I get to say what we do."
- "I make all the money, so you have to do what I say."

Often we try to take control of the relationship to minimize the potential of pain. Of course, that never works. The presence of power struggles actually increases the pain, but neither individual can see how they are contributing to the problem. Instead, they try even harder to gain control. Eventually the relationship begins a toxic spiral.

Power struggles within a relationship have a devastating effect:

- They separate friends. A couple is supposed to walk hand in hand through life. Friendship is born of equality; it's a relationship between peers. When power struggles occur, friends are separated. One has power and the other doesn't, which prevents the shared experience friendship demands. No longer do we respect and admire one another as equals. Instead, we demean and disrespect each other in an attempt to gain power.

- They alienate partners. In a healthy marriage, we have each other's back. We protect one another from a plethora of external threats. When power struggles appear, internal threats become more of a concern than external ones. The very people who are supposed to protect us threaten to injure us. This alienates us. We have to spend so much time worrying about the motives of one another that we have no ability to trust each other.

- They kill intimacy. As the struggle for power increases, the presence of trust decreases. Where there is no trust, true intimacy cannot be present. We might continue to have sex, but even sex can be a tool to gain power. It might be withheld or demanded as an attempt to control the other person. Each of us loses sight of giving pleasure to the other and makes sex all about ourselves. No matter the amount of physical contact, intimacy is absent.

Thankfully, there is a simple solution to power struggles. It isn't easy, but it is simple. Giving and receiving mercy within marriage destroys any struggle for power. Where power struggles exist, mercy does not. Where mercy is present, the struggle for power is absent.

Within marriage, mercy is the recognition of our imperfections and the willingness to choose loving actions no matter what we feel or what our spouse has done. The gift of mercy does not free us from all the consequences of our decisions, but it does release us from any debt owed to our spouse because of our choices.

Mercy empowers us to:

- support our spouse's well-being even if they haven't supported our own
- act in love toward our spouse even if their words or actions haven't been lovable
- have a deep empathy and compassion for the humanness of our spouse
- realize how often we make bad choices and understand others do the same
- refuse to manipulate or exploit our spouse for our own good
- reject the temptation to act out of fear or try to protect our own hearts
- experience friendship, partnership, and intimacy with our spouse over control
- speak kindly and with restraint to our spouse
- keep disagreements on topic and not stray into past issues
- attack problems together rather than use problems as an opportunity to attack one another
- confront problems rather than living in denial or overlooking them
- extend grace far beyond any human reason

When couples choose to give and receive mercy, the struggle for power disappears and a meaningful relationship grows.

Though growth requires participation from both spouses, it can start with just one spouse choosing mercy.

How to Have an Easy Marriage

Marriage looks easy. Nearly anyone can do it. You don't need permission. Anyone of age who can find a few dollars can get a license. Lessons aren't required and a competency test isn't given (although we should consider these).

But marriage isn't easy once we walk up the aisle as husband and wife. When we talk about two becoming one, we generally believe the "one" will be exactly like us. Rarely does our spouse agree. Instead, the two of us have to figure out which part of each other we are going to become. It's a perfect recipe for conflict.

Early marriage often finds difficulty from two sources:

1. *Lack of experience.* Competency is only gained through trial and error. When a couple gets married for the first time, neither are skilled at marriage. The natural inability that should exist is bound to create conflict.
2. *Differing expectations.* Without conscious thought, we all naturally respond to life the way our parents modeled for us. Not only do we respond as we have been taught, we assume others will respond the same way. The only problem is our spouse has been raised with a different model.

We generally believe we will take the model we grew up with, keep the good, throw out the bad, and make a few adaptations to create the perfect family. It's well intended, but it's foolish. It sounds like a good plan, but it's impossible.

When the original plan fails, many couples panic. Some assume they have married the wrong person and make plans to try again. Some search for satisfaction in another form—having a better job, a child, or some material possession. Some attempt to manipulate or coerce their spouse into who they want them to be. Some avoid conflict at all costs.

Yet when the original plan fails is when successful couples find the path to an easy marriage:

- They recognize their ignorance.
- They confess their expectations.
- They look beyond themselves for answers.
- They spend years learning about themselves, their spouses, and how best to operate.
- They read books, attend seminars, and seek input from anyone who has authority on the subject.
- They try and fail. They try and succeed. They seek forgiveness and give forgiveness.

Then, after a lifetime of learning, one day they wake up and realize that marriage is no longer a lot of work. This is because the energy spent trying to understand one another, make peace with one another, navigate the day-to-day operations of a relationship, and love one another has become an ingrained habit of joy.

Mercy is a salve that must be applied every day along that journey so that the process doesn't become too overwhelming. Without mercy, the journey might be too long. The pain would be too great. Our impatience would set in and we would give up. Many do. Most likely that happens because they aren't doing the work necessary while continually receiving and giving mercy to one another.

An easy marriage is possible. It just doesn't happen the way people expect. It's a by-product of a lifetime of love, not an immediate gift to those who say "I do."

> **PRACTICING THE COMMITMENT** Mercy is a long-suffering, undeserved love. Challenge each other to show mercy five times in the next week to someone in your life. When someone responds harshly to a social media post, refuse to reply with equal harshness. Instead, soften the conversation. Identify someone who has frustrated or hurt you in the past and find a way to do something nice for them. Find someone who is hurting and go out of your way to assist them by bringing them a meal or doing a household chore on their behalf.
>
> At the end of the week, go to dinner as a couple and discuss your five acts of mercy. What was it like? How did you want to respond? What surprised you?

A Misconception about Mercy

There is a major misconception when it comes to mercy. Many people assume it's a weak feeling when it's actually a tough action. While mercy might begin with a compassionate heart, it isn't mercy unless it's an action. We can't be merciful in spirit unless we are merciful in deed. We don't *feel* mercy; we *do* mercy.

Mercy is the activity of a grace that is felt. It's the hands and feet of grace. Both *mercy* and *grace* connote a person in power having compassion on someone under their control. Grace is feeling compassion; mercy is acting on it. Grace gives us the eyes to see someone in the midst of struggle and have compassion on them. Mercy causes us to join them in their misery with the hopes of alleviating it, if by no other means than by simply giving them company.

Mercy is enacted when something happens that could give one spouse power over the other. A husband speaks harshly to his wife. It's clearly a mistake, and apart from mercy, that mistake gives the wife power over her husband. She can remind him of his error and excuse her bad actions because of his behavior. This gives her the upper hand. But when mercy is present, she refuses to use that power. She forgives and doesn't hold his mistake over him. Her forgiveness doesn't relieve him of his responsibilities—recognizing the mistake, apologizing, making amends, and learning. But it does release him from her grip. Her refusal to use the situation against him is mercy.

Mercy is an action of strength. It's cowardice to ignore a spouse's rude behavior and pretend like it didn't happen. Fear says, "If I bring it up, he won't love me," or experience says, "I better not rock the boat." Mercy isn't denial. Mercy recognizes the wrong, names it, and offers forgiveness, but refuses to keep record of the wrong. It is never used to shame or guilt another. In no way is the offending spouse seen as evil or less than human.

It's easy to hold a grudge. Using our spouse's weakness against them can feel more productive. We think it will protect us when our mistakes are revealed. But it takes courage to forgive. It's a brave act to recognize and admit our own faults so that we are more gracious with the faults of others. Mercy is not some fragile feeling. It's a strong action that is most often avoided because it demands too much from us.

Failing to understand that mercy is strong leads to an equal mistake—believing tenderness and toughness cannot coexist. Mercy requires toughness to restrain the desire of revenge, and it requires tenderness to have empathy and compassion for another person. The best marriages are defined by both toughness and tenderness. These couples have a backbone. There is a deep strength that empowers them. They have the courage to face the truth, admit frustrations, have difficult conversations, endure the hardships of life, and face whatever comes their way. They also have a tenderness toward each other, the sorrows of others, and the hurting and hopeless. Those who are truly tough have the courage to be tender. Those who are willing to be tender must be tough.

When thinking of the qualities that lead to a lasting relationship, few people would ever consider mercy. Yet anyone who has ever experienced a truly meaningful relationship can reflect on and realize the influence mercy had on their union. As fallen people who live in a fallen world, we are continually in need of mercy—undeserved, unearned, with nothing expected in return. Couples who have the ability to receive and give mercy, without ever taking advantage of the kindness of their spouse, have every opportunity to be successful in marriage. For those who don't have the courage to forgive or who are unwilling to risk mercy, marriage will forever be a struggle of power, control, one-upmanship, paranoia, and fear. Mercy creates the climate in which a marriage can work.

BE INTENTIONAL

1. Why do power struggles occur in marriage? How do those struggles strain our relationships?

2. How does mercy express itself in a healthy marriage?

3. Of the characteristics of mercy listed on page 120, which ones need to be added to your relationship?

4. How is mercy more a sign of strength than weakness?

COMMITMENT 6

HAPPILY LIVE IN TRUTH

When we are completely committed to one another, have promised to love one another in every circumstance, are *for* one another in tangible ways, and are willing to sacrifice our own desires to assist one another, marriage is a place where the truth flourishes.

If you can't tell your spouse the truth, you have a problem. It may not cause divorce. It doesn't guarantee your relationship is bad. You may not even be able to feel the negative effects on your marriage. But it is a problem.

By nature, humans lie. It's not a learned behavior. It just happens. From an early age, we believe deception is better than truth. While it can be cute when a two-year-old says they haven't eaten anything even as remnants of an Oreo cookie are all over their face, it's not as cute when a husband conceals his whereabouts or a wife says she is "fine" even when she is not.

Lies kill. They may not end the whole relationship, but they destroy elements of trust, intimacy, and connection. Where a lie reigns, a true relationship does not. Unless we are interacting based on the truth, we are not truly relating to one another.

Spouses lie for several reasons:

1. We have something to hide. Either we've chosen horrific actions that rightly would threaten the state of our relationship if they were found out, or we have wrongly concluded that any exposed weakness would be a hindrance to a healthy marriage. Whichever is the case, we work diligently to hide our failures and keep the appearance of perfection.

2. We don't feel safe. Having expressed the truth in the past and experienced a bad response in return, many of us lie because we are afraid of how the other person will respond. While love breeds safety, any doubt of the fullness of our spouse's love will lead to insecurity. Lies are often a sign that safety is not present.

3. We think our spouse isn't worth it. The truth can hurt. It can cause tension and reveal problems. If we do not value our marriage or our spouse, it can be easier to lie. Why have the serious discussion when a lie can avoid it? Why reveal our true heart if we don't really love our spouse? When we value our spouse, the difficult conversation is always worth it because we're in it for the long haul. But when we don't value our spouse, we might be more worried with how we feel today than with what happens tomorrow.

4. We think *we* aren't worth it. We believe if our spouse sees who we truly are, they will not (and even cannot) love us, because we do not think we are valuable. The sadness of this lie is that it robs our spouse of the opportunity of giving us grace and true love. Over time, we can actually begin to believe they are not loving us well, never realizing we have taken from them any opportunity to express their love.

5. We think we need to control our spouse. Many lies are not attempts to protect ourselves but an attempt to control others. We tell people what we want to tell them, expecting them to react the way we think they should. In a healthy marriage, one spouse doesn't try to control the other, as both individuals are free to be themselves. In an unhealthy marriage, manipulation and control are commonplace.

6. We don't know any different. Some people are taught from a very early age to lie, and they know of no other way to be in a relationship. Because lying is all they've seen, it's all they know, so it's all they do. Unfortunately, this prevents them from ever having a true relationship. Anything built on a lie is a world that does not truly exist. Until the lies stop, a healthy relationship cannot grow.

Truth Is a Learned Skill

We can learn to handle the truth. We can build a pattern of truth telling so that a deep level of trust is created. As we repeatedly tell the truth, we will see how truth telling liberates the relationship and frees us from many underlying motives—manipulation, masking feelings, hypocrisy, etc. As we tell the truth and humbly hear the truth, we can create a climate where the truth defines who we are.

In his book *The Meaning of Marriage*, Timothy Keller writes, "One of the most basic skills in marriage is the ability to tell the straight, unvarnished truth about what your spouse has done—and then, completely, unself-righteously, and joyously express forgiveness without a shred of superiority, without making the other person feel small."[1]

Keller's words show a clear pattern for truth telling and mirror what we've learned from the lucky ones. A marriage in which the truth is regularly told requires humility. Both spouses must realize their imperfections and expect them from themselves and their spouse. They may never overestimate their ability or consider themselves better than the other.

Truth telling is evidence that mercy is present. It is more likely to be present when a couple has a shared purpose. Unless the marriage is about more than just personal pleasure, truth has very little chance of being a defining characteristic. When a couple sees their relationship as having a higher purpose (contributing to the communal good, impacting children, influencing society, bringing glory to God), they are more likely to do the hard work of learning to tell the truth.

Lies Never to Tell Your Spouse

While all lies hurt a marriage, four specific lies commonly cause the most damage.

Lies of location. Except for the possible planning of a surprise party or trip, I should never have to lie to my wife about where I have been or where I am going. Lying about either of these issues reveals an area of my life in which I am intentionally trying to cut out my wife. She is the most important person in my life. Cutting her out can only be done for negative reasons.

Lies of communication. My wife should be aware of every form of communication available to me. I should never have a secret email account or an unknown cell phone number. While my job requires certain elements of confidentiality, I do not hide who I'm speaking with. There is no reason to have secret conversations with others that my wife cannot find out about.

Lies of location and communication are the two greatest warning signs of adultery. If you find your spouse lying about either, make an appointment with a counselor.

Lies of finance. One of the most surprising elements of doing funerals over the past decade is the number of unknown loans, debts, bank accounts, and other financial issues that come out after someone's death. I had never known the number of people who make secret transactions without the knowledge or consent of their spouse. A financial lie is often a lie of extreme childishness. Unwilling or unable to find common ground with our spouse over a financial decision, we act like an eight-year-old and steal the cookie when we think no one is looking. Instead of lying, we need to work on communication and negotiation. If both of us still cannot agree on a purchase, we don't make the purchase.

Lies of feelings. The most common lies seem innocent. Saying "I don't care" when you actually do. Saying "That's fine" when it's actually not. These lies conceal how we truly feel. It's never our job to read the mind of our spouse. Loving someone doesn't mean we have the ability to predict how they feel at every moment. Communication is necessary. If we do not tell the truth about what we think and how we feel, true intimacy cannot take place. Lying about feelings reveals that we don't trust our spouse enough to show them who we actually are. It's a warning sign of a relationship that isn't as healthy as it might appear. True intimacy allows us to reveal our actual selves to our spouse and know we will be loved.

We lie because we think lying is easier. It will get us what we want without anyone being hurt. And it often works . . . for a time. Yet eventually lies are discovered. Hearts are hurt. Relationships are broken. Trust is shattered. Lying might be easier in the moment, but it's more difficult in the long haul.

That's why it is vital to tell the truth. Even when it's hard. Even when it's not convenient. Even when you think you can get away with a lie.

One of the responsibilities of marriage is to tell the truth. It might be difficult in the moment, but it will pay great rewards over a lifetime. Good marriages are built on the truth.

Truth Purifies

The alternative to a culture of lies is a purity of heart. Notice it's "purity of heart," not "perfection of heart." If perfection is the standard, not one of us has a hope for a healthy marriage. But purity of heart is possible. The pure in heart are those who live in the truth. They aren't deceiving themselves into thinking they are something more than what they are. They aren't hiding from their spouse, pretending to be one thing but actually being something else. They aren't putting on a facade for others, acting as though they have a great marriage when they really do not. Instead, they seek, acknowledge, and live by the truth. When our hearts are pure, we believe in the power of truth.

This life-giving truth begins with an understanding of God's presence in their lives. They recognize his authority and creative design. They know marriage was his idea long before it was theirs. They believe that to best understand it, they must seek God's wisdom regarding how marriage is to work.

The truth overflows into every area of their relationship. They try to identify lies they have believed about success, happiness, meaning, and value. They recognize society is regularly telling them a false story of how to experience true intimacy. They are aware that just because something was their experience growing up doesn't mean it is the only way or the best way to do things. They seek wisdom from others and knowledge from experts on how to best relate to their spouse.

For the pure in heart, truth is a continual pursuit in every aspect of life. Because they are poor in spirit, they know their own temptations. Because they regularly mourn, they aren't deceived into thinking they are perfect. Because they are meek, they use their strength to see truth together with their spouse. Because they hunger and thirst for righteousness, they are not satisfied to live in a lie. Because they receive and give mercy, they are patient with themselves and others as they seek the truth. And the truth is a continual pursuit because they believe it really is the source of connection.

Apart from intentional deception, there are two main temptations that lead to an impurity of heart. The first is hypocrisy. If there is any place where hypocrisy should not be present, it's in marriage. When we commit to love one another no matter the circumstances, we are free to put down the masks and reveal our true selves. But often we are afraid to do so. We are neither good at showing our real selves nor good at seeing the full view of another person. We have been so trained to cover our weakness for fear it might be exploited by others that we naturally hide aspects of our lives even from those we love. The hiding creates hypocrisy. Our spouse believes they know us completely when we are actually keeping part of our heart from them.

Until we reveal the totality of who we are to our spouse, we are not fully loving them as we should. We are holding out. That's not fair to them because we aren't giving them the chance to love every part of us. It's not fair to us because we are rejecting love in the places that likely need it the most.

The second threat to having a pure heart is denial. Whether we intentionally don't believe the truth or we fail to do the work to learn the truth, we are living in denial. Denial expresses itself in a variety of ways in marriage:

- pretending an addiction isn't that big of a problem
- ignoring our need to save for retirement
- staying silent on an issue that is greatly frustrating
- blaming our spouse for every problem in the relationship
- ignoring obvious signs of betrayal
- acting as though a problem is solved by one conversation when we know it's not
- saying yes when we mean no
- minimizing our feelings or the consequences of our actions
- justifying bad behavior

However denial presents itself, it threatens the purity of the marriage. Even if both parties prefer denial over the truth, they are choosing to live in a lie. While the lie might feel more comfortable, it is not a true relationship. We are connecting with the lie, not with one another.

Denial is often what makes an affair possible. One or both parties engaging in the affair are living in denial. They have justified their actions, likely blamed their spouse for a poor relationship, and are pretending as though the adulterous relationship is real even though it isn't. They compare the fantasy of an affair (no responsibility and an easy emotional/physical connection) to the reality of a marriage (full of responsibilities, difficult decisions and conversations, and common frustrations). Of course the affair looks and feels better. It's like comparing an airbrushed model on a magazine cover to the actual person.

The problem with hypocrisy and denial is that they can become comfortable. We often use these two defense mechanisms not because we are evil but because we are afraid. It's our cowardice that drives us to lie. Yet if we would tell ourselves the truth and have the courage to live by the truth, our marriage would reap the reward.

Truth Breeds Intimacy

For the average man, the words *intimacy* and *sex* are synonyms. We can't separate the two. This often frustrates women. Not understanding how our minds think of the two identically, many women wrongly conclude, "All you want is sex," when in reality what the husband wants is intimacy.

Most women have a better ability to distinguish between the two. While sex can be intimate, intimacy can happen without sex, and sex can happen in a way that isn't intimate. The Hebrew word often used in the Old Testament to describe sex is the word *yada*. It means "to know." The phrase "yada, yada, yada" literally means "you know, you know, you know." In the Hebrew mindset, to have sex with someone was to know them. This concept was more apparent in a society where little interaction took place between the sexes and where even the appearance of a woman was veiled from every man except her husband. Sex was the moment in which a woman was fully seen . . . fully known.

This is the true meaning of intimacy within marriage—to be fully loved and deeply known. I want to say "fully known," but to know someone fully is not possible. Our knowledge is always limited, and the object of our affection is always changing. We can never know fully, but we can know deeply. And we can always be pursuing to know more.

The unseen cost of hypocrisy and denial is a destruction of intimacy. The by-product of having purity of heart is that we know one another better, and that knowledge can lead to a deeper intimacy. When we hide parts of who we are, we are robbing our marriage of true connection.

Why Intimacy Wanes

For many couples, intimacy in their relationship is failing not because of lack of sex but because of lack of knowledge. They don't know each other. Whether through apathy or intentional withholding, they have stopped paying attention to the intricate details of one another:

- How does she order her salad?
- What are his busiest seasons of the year?
- What stresses her out about work?
- How can she help him in the most meaningful way at home?
- Where does he like to sit in a restaurant?
- What are the important days or occasions in each other's lives?
- What is his favorite TV show?
- What song cheers her up?

These are the things of intimacy. For a couple to know these details and to use that knowledge for the betterment of their spouse is true intimacy. While they should not expect their spouse to know everything about them, it is a fair expectation that their spouse will know them better than anyone else does.

For most couples, this knowledge comes naturally in the early stages of a relationship. Many early dates are spent asking and answering questions. Both partners are on high alert to understand one another. They each study to see who the other is and what they like.

With time, however, the natural interest can fade. Couples can get complacent in their knowledge. Many times they fail to understand that they each continue to change. Slowly their knowledge turns to ignorance and their intimacy fades.

Hindrances to Intimate Knowledge

It is a basic human desire to be known. We want another person to fully see us. We desire to be known and loved. Yet we often fail to know or be known. This happens for two reasons.

Fear. Even while we desire to be known, we are terrified. From our earliest moments, we are taught to conceal our true selves. We hide so our weaknesses are not exploited. For many people, the desire to be known is never greater than the fear of what might happen if someone truly sees who we are. If we're unwilling to let down our guard and show our true hearts, our spouse has no chance of knowing us. No matter how hard they try, they cannot know us if we do not make ourselves known.

Laziness. To know another person takes effort. We must make cognitive space for another person. If the brain is like a computer, we must have a folder on our spouse and continually put files into that folder. This is an ongoing process. While most partners begin the process, many grow lazy in the relationship. We stop trying, unwilling to do the work, and our knowledge begins to fade. No matter how courageous our spouse may be in revealing their heart, they will not be known if we aren't paying attention.

Fear prevents us from being known; laziness prevents us from knowing.

How to Renew Intimacy

While intimate knowledge is quickly lost, it can be regained. Nearly every couple will go through seasons where they have failed to pay proper attention to what is going on in the life of their spouse. Healthy couples recognize the pattern and change. Unhealthy couples apathetically continue down the path of ignorance. We can regain intimate knowledge of our spouse by:

- *Choosing to care.* We won't learn if we don't care. It's a conscious decision to study our spouse in order to love them well. Until we decide this is a valuable pursuit, all other steps will be useless.
- *Paying attention.* Much of knowledge comes from properly seeing our spouse and then doing the work to store what we see. By paying attention to their actions and words, we can grow in our understanding of who they are.
- *Spending a quantity of quality time together.* Knowledge can come only with time. When we fail to spend meaningful time with our spouse, our understanding of them will diminish. By intentionally choosing to spend important time with them, we can better know them.
- *Being brave.* It takes courage to reveal ourselves to another . . . even our spouse. Yet the willingness is often worth it. If our spouse has proven themselves trustworthy, we can have the courage to take a step in revealing more about ourselves to them.
- *Asking, not assuming.* A great danger for older couples is that we assume we already know our spouse. Instead of assuming, ask their opinion. Investigate their interests. We can test our assumptions to see if they are accurate. We learn about each other the way we learn anything—through questions and answers.

True intimacy is to be fully loved and deeply known. It's a knowledge that might include sex, but it is a far broader topic than just sex.

> **PRACTICING THE COMMITMENT** To live in truth, we must know the truth about our spouse. We know those we love and we love those we know.
>
> Create ten questions about yourself that your spouse should be able to answer but probably can't. Who are your two best friends? What is your biggest fear? What is your greatest stress this week? After each of you have created your ten questions, exchange tests and write down your answers. Who knows the other better? What questions did you get wrong? What did you learn about your partner?

Purity Drives Rather Than Drifts

While couples might be tempted to run from the truth, as they learn to live in it, they begin to be drawn together. When they increase their proximity to one another, it can lead to a climate where they are more likely to reveal themselves and live by the truth.

Proximity matters. In healthy marriages, couples devise ways to spend more time near one another. In unhealthy marriages, couples subconsciously drift away from one another. Proximity is both a cause and an effect of marital satisfaction.

Few things forge friendships as much as proximity. Consider your first friend. I can almost guarantee you that person either lived next door or was in your first grade class. In the beginning of dating relationships, a couple spends more and more time with one another as the attraction grows. Being physically close to one another increases the likelihood of a shared positive experience, which bonds two people together and gives them an appreciation for one another. The more positive interactions a couple has, the less powerful a negative interaction will be.

A healthy marriage does not necessarily have fewer negative interactions than an unhealthy marriage. It may experience the same amount. However, because a healthy couple has so many more positive interactions than a couple who is struggling, the negative moments do not have the same impact on their perception or feelings.

An absence of regular proximity robs the couple of the opportunity of having more meaningful shared experiences. It diminishes conversation, lessens laughter, and puts added pressure on the rare times the couple is together.

If you want to feel closer to your spouse, get closer to them. By sharing time, experience, and space, you are more likely to have empathy, understanding, and a common perspective.

The Dangers of Proximity

Proximity is so powerful regarding relationships that married couples must guard against others sharing what is meant for them alone. While boundaries must be present with everyone, special attention must be given to those people who work around us or live near us. It's no coincidence coworkers often cross boundary lines and act in inappropriate ways. Proximity can nourish a wrong relationship just as easily as it can assist a right relationship.

We must recognize the dangers of proximity and be on guard against making foolish choices. Consider the neighbors, co-workers, clients, friends, workout partners, coaches, and any person of the opposite sex with whom you will be in close proximity. Don't run from those relationships, but do recognize they present a unique temptation that deserves extra attention. Strong boundaries can protect you while allowing the relationships to be healthy.

The Opportunities of Proximity

Being near one another creates a great opportunity for spouses. By intentionally finding ways to be close to one another, a couple can increase the likelihood of meaningful connection. Intention isn't necessary early in a relationship. Proximity happens naturally. No one has to tell an engaged couple to spend time together. Very few newlyweds struggle to be near one another. But as time passes, kids arrive, and the responsibilities of life increase, a couple's proximity can either be stolen from them or slowly drift away.

Especially during a few specific seasons of marriage (chasing toddlers, chauffeuring children, and raising teenagers), most couples have to find ways to be near one another. If they don't, they run the risk of slowly drifting from one another. For example:

- He doesn't like what she's watching on TV, so he goes to another room.
- Two kids have different events on the same night, so each parent goes a different direction.
- She stays up late while he goes to bed early.
- She sleeps in while he leaves for the office.

It doesn't take much of this before a couple who used to spend a lot of time close to one another is rarely in the same room alone. The lack of proximity comes with a price. The consequences are rarely noticed. But over time a couple can feel their closeness slipping. They might say, "We're growing apart" or "I feel like we don't even know each other anymore." What they don't realize is that as they have physically spent less time in one another's presence, it's taken an emotional and spiritual toll.

The average couple can benefit greatly from making intentional choices to be in closer proximity. Here are some intentional ways to get closer to each other:

- Have a family dinner. One of the best ways for a whole family to get closer to one another is to form the habit of eating at least one meal a day together. It's not always easy, but the commitment is worth it.

- Take a vacation. Sometimes you need to reset your relationship. Getting away from the daily responsibilities, routines, and children can reconnect a couple in a powerful way. Being together in a car or on a plane can reintroduce spouses to each other. Spending a week or weekend in a different place can force a couple to communicate more with one another than with others.

- Touch. Nonsexual touch is a wonderful way to feel closer to your spouse. Obviously to touch your spouse you must be near them, but a touch also causes them to recognize your nearness.

- Live in a smaller house. Less space can force a couple to be nearer to one another. Too many couples buy a house without ever considering its possible impact on their relationship. A bigger house requires even more attention to making sure you are spending time together.

- Choose to be closer. The most important step to feeling closer is simply choosing to be closer. Instead of physically separating from your spouse, make the decision to stay near them. Don't go to a separate room to relax. Don't pick up your phone when you first go to bed. Do sit near your spouse when watching TV.

This isn't to say a couple always needs to be by one another's side. Distance is also an important part of a healthy relationship. Each individual must maintain their personal identity apart from the marriage, and sometimes they need to get away from one another in order to get close. But most couples are spending enough time apart. They aren't spending enough time together.

Proximity matters in marriage. But there is one warning—proximity helps a relationship only if it doesn't highlight repulsive attributes of a spouse. Some relationships will get worse if a couple increases their proximity because one or both spouses detest aspects of their husband or wife. In these cases, proximity reveals a deeper problem. If increasing your proximity to your spouse makes your relationship worse, get help immediately.

In a marriage where each spouse seeks a pure heart and the heart of the relationship is kept pure, the couple will see one another. They will see the fullness of their spouse. They won't fixate on problems, but they also won't be in denial, thinking their spouse is perfect. They won't believe their relationship is without flaws, and they won't be overwhelmed by the challenges they face. They will see each other as flawed but loved.

Purity of heart allows for true intimacy in a marriage.

BE **INTENTIONAL**

1. What is the relationship between truth and intimacy?

2. How do small lies hinder intimacy? Why do they distance spouses from each other?

3. Why are we afraid of the truth? How can we overcome our fears?

4. How can you increase your proximity to your spouse?

COMMITMENT 7

HAPPILY MAKE PEACE

In my first book, *Friends, Partners, and Lovers*, I wrote about Nelson Mandela, Henry Kissinger, Kofi Annan, and Shimon Peres. This diverse group shares two things in common—each won the Nobel Peace Prize and each was divorced.

These four were able to make peace in situations where it seemed impossible, yet none of them could make lasting peace with their wives. They were able to navigate the subtle dance of international diplomacy but were not able to figure out how to lie in bed at night with the same woman for a lifetime.

Alfred Nobel, the founder of the Nobel Prize, was never able to find a lasting relationship. Two of the three negotiators of the Treaty of Versailles, which ended World War I, were divorced.

It seems like a great irony, yet Nobel Peace laureates have the same disagreements and stalemates as the rest of us—pastors and factory workers, salesmen and saleswomen, doctors and lawyers.

From Complementary to Competitive

Amid all the flowers and pictures, the big promises and youthful excitement of a wedding, something else is taking place—the beginning of the discovery of just how different we are from our spouse.

When a man and woman come together in holy matrimony, it appears like a loving union between two completely compatible individuals who will live in peace and love. In many ways that's true. Love, respect, and enjoyment of each other's company define many marriages. However, it is also true that marriage is a collision of two adversarial beings who have different desires, mindsets, expectations, and backgrounds, as well as a history of fear, betrayal, and hurt.

It wasn't always this way. When God created humanity in Genesis 1–2, he intended us to complement one another.[1] We were created differently for a reason. It made us better.

Studies have shown an interesting thing about happily married couples—we are twice as knowledgeable.[2] It's not that smarter couples have better marriages; it's that happy couples subconsciously know if their spouse is going to remember something or if they need to remember it. Marriage is like a second hard drive on a computer. I can store something on my hard drive or I can store it on Jenny's. There is no need for me to remember many of the things she can remember. How often do you find yourself asking your spouse some piece of information? They have stored it so you don't have to. (I think this is one reason I always have to ask Jenny how long it will take to warm up something in the microwave.)

Storing information is just one example of how men and women were made to complement each other. Yet when sin entered the world, the differences that were supposed to unite us divided us. The characteristics that were supposed to complement irritated.

Notice one of the first effects of sin in Genesis 3 is that the couple who was made for each other was divided in blame. God asked Adam what had happened, and Adam blamed Eve for his actions. Instead of taking joint responsibility and locking arms in humility before God, Adam and Eve attempted to separate themselves from each other.

Thousands of years later, couples do the same—blaming one another, fighting with one another, seeing the other spouse as the problem instead of seeing them as a partner to help solve the problem. If we aren't careful, entering into a relationship with someone so different than us can draw out our natural tendencies to protect ourselves, to fight, to be war makers.

Peacemaking versus Peace-Receiving

Notice the term is *peacemaking*, not *peace-receiving*. Making peace requires effort. It's a job. It's a task that ensures great struggle, failure, and frustration. Peace is not simply bestowed onto relationships; it is fought for. If peace was simply received, we could step back and wait for it to come. If it never did, we could switch spouses, assuming the lack of peace was a sign we chose the wrong partner. Yet peace is not received; it's made. Issues are confronted, wills are tested, humility is required, and soul searching and compromise are demanded.

Peacemaking is one of our most important roles in marriage. If we understand the connection between marriage and peacemaking, we will expect conflict and be prepared for it. However, if we ignore the connection, we can be lured into thinking conflict is abnormal, a sign of incompatibility, or evidence the relationship isn't working.

Peacemaking, not peace-receiving, is an aspect of every healthy marriage. Making peace may be the hardest work there is, requiring all the skill and ability we possess. But it's also some of the most important work we do.

Characteristics of True Peace

True peacemaking is defined by several characteristics. It requires that each person feels heard. This doesn't simply mean each person has a chance to speak. They can speak and not be heard. For someone to be heard, ideas must be processed and contemplated. The person must be seen and respected. I can submit to any leader and their decision if I trust them and they have heard me. Within a respected marriage relationship, we can agree to most resolutions if we are heard.

However, it is not enough to be heard; true peacemaking requires being understood as well. Understanding requires another person to look at the issue from our perspective, experience, and background. Understanding gives us the feeling of being known. Someone can repeat back to us everything we have said and the tone with which we said it, but they still may not have understood us. Without being understood, we cannot feel as though we play an active role in the outcome. Marriage psychologist John Gottman says, "Human nature dictates that it is virtually impossible to accept advice from someone unless you feel that the person understands you."[3]

PRACTICING THE COMMITMENT The speaker/listener technique is a common tool used to build understanding. Grab a tennis ball, find a quiet place, and discuss one aspect of your marriage with your spouse. Begin by holding the ball and giving a brief description of how you feel about the issue. After sharing a small chunk of information, throw the ball to your spouse. They then paraphrase what they have heard. They don't rebut, interject how they feel, or judge what they have heard; they simply paraphrase what they heard and throw the ball back. When you receive the ball, you can validate the paraphrase or recommunicate the original point until it is properly expressed. When you feel fully understood on the issue, the process can begin again with your spouse sharing their feelings and you paraphrasing what you hear.[4]

Being a part of the resolution is a requirement for peace. True peace is not the result of being dictated to or forced into an agreement. Playing a contributing role to a resolution leads to lasting peace.

Notice true peace doesn't mean agreement. It is assumed that successful marriages solve every conflict, but according to Gottman's research, 69 percent of marital problems are perpetual problems.[5] The difference between success and failure in marriage is not agreeing on every issue but accepting that some issues will not be resolved.

Healthy relationships can actually be strengthened by differing opinions. They cause both spouses to remember they might be wrong, realize there is another way to see the issue, and show sensitivity to those who hold opposing views. If agreement was necessary on every issue, each individual would be forced to lose their identity, stripping them of one of their greatest strengths—diversity of thought and perspective.

Peace is not the result of agreement but finding an acceptance in the differences. Ironically, we can agree with someone and not have peace while we can disagree with someone but still have true peace. An aspect of peace is resolution, but knowing a problem cannot be settled is actually a type of resolution. Acceptance of an issue communicates about more than just the issue; it also communicates acceptance of a person—their beliefs, behaviors, opinions, and experiences.

Counterfeits to Peace

There are several counterfeits to peace that look like the real thing but in the end are a bad alternative. Having never experienced true peace or not being willing to do the work to accomplish true peace, we can be deceived into thinking these counterfeits are real.

One counterfeit to peace is pacifism. Fearing the discomfort of conflict or the fear of rejection, some take a pacifist approach to disagreements. The result can look like peace, but it is a pseudo-peace that appears good on the outside yet doesn't contain the true elements of peace on the inside. Pacifists are taken advantage of, are run over, and must deny their own opinions, ideas, and beliefs in order to give the appearance of peace.

A problem with pacifism is that few people are truly pacifists. They might refuse war, but they are willing to wage a war of words with those who disagree with them. A wife may refuse to stand up to her husband, but she fights back by withholding intimacy or manipulating to get her way. A husband might take the way of the pacifist when it comes to sharing emotions, but he pouts his way into getting what he wants in other areas. Pacifism is a counterfeit because true marital peace is found when both spouses fully engage in finding a workable resolution to a problem. Without both parties involved, true peace is not found.

Another counterfeit, bullying, can give the appearance of peace. Many bullies believe they have healthy marriages because they always get what they want. This may look like peace, but it is far from it. In the same way that pacifism takes one of the partners out of the equation by their own consent, bullying forces one of the partners out of the equation without their consent. Many bullies are shocked to realize their spouse is not happy because they have confused a lack of conflict for peace.

A third type of counterfeit peace is avoidance. Avoidance comes in two expressions—denial of difficulty or a feeling that trying to confront the difficulty isn't worth it. Jim Collins, in his book *Good to Great*, describes great companies who "confront the brutal facts yet never lose faith."[6] A good marriage must do both of these things. We must confront the brutal facts so we do not live in denial of who we are, yet we must never lose faith that we can improve and withstand whatever comes our way. When we lose this ability, we avoid difficult issues, either denying they exist because we have fallen in love with the image of a perfect marriage, or fearing if an issue is confronted our marriage is not strong enough to withstand the conflict. True peace is only found when we do not avoid issues but face them head-on and with a trust in our spouse that our bond is stronger than the conflict.

Realizing our weaknesses and imperfections drives us to action. It reminds us every relationship will contain imperfections, and we are the cause of many of those. It breeds humility, which will prevent us from accepting a counterfeit to peace and make us open to change.

Having mourned our sin will acquaint us with the brutal facts of our situation before God and enable us to face any issue no matter the difficulty. It empowers us to be gracious to our spouse even if they are wrong, and it makes us quick to admit when we are wrong. Mourning tempers our attitudes and actions, making us less likely to stand our ground no matter what the situation.

Meekness confronts all three forms of false peace. It prevents us from apathy, which avoids the problem or causes pacifism, but it also tempers our actions so that we do not bully others and strip our spouse of their personhood. Meekness causes us to face issues but not force them.

Knowing that marriage is bigger than us puts any issue at hand in its proper context, submitting its importance to the greater good of the lasting relationship. It causes the pacifist to recognize some fights are worth having; it causes the avoider to face issues as a way toward transformation; and it prevents the bully from winning an argument at the cost of the higher call of the relationship.

Mercy creates a climate in which disagreement can take place with safety. It is received so the avoider can have courage to act. It is given so the bully will not force their opinion. The nature of mercy reminds the pacifist that it takes effort to give and receive mercy.

Valuing truth prevents us from acting out of sinfulness and protecting a deeper issue. Sometimes pacifism, avoidance, and bullying are a ploy to cover other problems. The bully rages in anger lest he open his heart and reveal the sinful condition he is hiding. The pacifist is walked on, hoping no one will notice her and her struggles.

Nothing enlightens us to the difficulty of this commitment as much as the one to follow. We would think that making peace would end all trouble, but a lucky couple not only has to make peace; they have to endure through criticism and opposition as they do the right things.

Safety

In their book *Crucial Confrontations*, Kerry Patterson and his coauthors say, "When there is enough safety, you can talk to almost anyone about almost anything."[7] They make a key point about the importance of safety, arguing that we should focus on the safety of the conversation before moving on to the reason for the confrontation. When we feel safe, we operate with great freedom to be ourselves, be influenced by others, and act in a gracious way. When safety is threatened, we become skeptical and territorial. The first step of the peacemaking process is creating a climate of safety.

Notice how the previous commitments have already offered this climate. If our relationship is defined by mercy, the climate of safety is already formed. We have an ability to be wrong, to forgive and be forgiven, and to know our hearts will not be exploited. When mercy is not present, there is no promise of forgiveness or safety in offering forgiveness to another; it appears dangerous to show weakness, fault, or uncertainty because that weakness may be exploited and used against us.

The human need for safety and our experiences of not being safe are one aspect that makes peacemaking so difficult. Even if someone is willing to try to become a peacemaker, they often get scared back into self-defense the first time it doesn't go well. Many spouses can recall an event that happened years ago and name it as the reason they don't dare confront issues. This history is why it is so important for new couples to begin the peacemaking process as soon as possible. The sooner those initial steps start, the faster trust can be built and the human tendency to handle conflict incorrectly can be thwarted.

Stones and Seeds

We live in a stone-throwing world. It's a world where everyone holds a stone; we throw first and ask questions later. Stones hurt. They damage to an extent that is difficult to repair. They don't discriminate—they will injure whoever is in their way.

The great danger of living in a world full of stones is it forces us to always be on the lookout. At any moment and from any direction, stones can come flying at us. In order to stay safe, we have to watch out for them.

Of course, as we look for stones, we see them. We often see whatever we expect to see. Psychologists call it *confirmation bias*. We seek, interpret, and remember information that confirms our thoughts more than information that changes our thoughts. This is why a political ally and a political enemy can do the same thing and we forgive the ally but revile the enemy. While we believe we look at others neutrally, we see everyone through the lens of a bias. It's why most political debates do not change minds as much as they confirm them. When we are biased toward expecting stones, we will see stones.

The opposite metaphor of a stone is a seed.[8] In James, the writer uses a seed as an illustration for peace: "And those who are peacemakers will plant seeds of peace and reap a harvest of righteousness" (3:18 NLT).

On its own, a seed is not very much. It is easily forgotten or overlooked. The power of the seed is in what it can become. With time, care, and the right conditions, a seed can become something very meaningful.

Peace is like a seed. It starts small and seems worthless, but over time it can grow into a harvest.

There are two options—a stone or a seed. Which do you choose? Are you throwing stones or planting seeds? Do you more often reach for the stone to protect yourself or your reputation, to make your point, to defend your side? Or do you more often plant seeds to build connection, to reassure of your love, to bring peace, to deflate the discussion?

Jesus calls us to be seed spreaders. To throw the seed of peace everywhere we can. Of course, not every seed will thrive, but the promise of James 3 is that if we sow the seed of peace we will reap a harvest of righteousness.

The bad news of humanity is that when given a choice between a seed and a stone, we will often choose a stone.

A stone gives the illusion of safety. No one can use a seed for safety.

The irony is a stone doesn't make us safer. It places us in more danger. The safety a stone promises is an illusion, yet we choose it all the time.

There is only one situation in which someone would choose a seed over a stone—if they felt completely safe and could take the risk of choosing a seed and what it could become.

Notice what God has done for us. He has promised us safety in his mercy. It is a mercy that comes underserved to us. It is a mercy that purifies our hearts and allows us to hope in him. Then we see God, and we see him at work all around us, which allows us to trust in him and drop our need to protect ourselves. We then have the courage to be like the God we see—a peacemaker.

A Peacemaker's Vision

Peacemaking only comes from a vision of God. When we see God, it changes how we see everything else. Peacemakers don't live in different worlds; they simply see better than the rest of us. They can detect opportunities for peace that we overlook. One of the greatest differences between a peacemaker and the rest of us is that while we are always looking for places of division, a peacemaker is always looking for places of unity.

Failed Repair Attempts

Marriage psychologist John Gottman is famous for being able to detect divorce with a 91 percent accuracy after just five minutes of conversation.[9] He looks for several signs, one of which he calls "failed repair attempts." As a conversation turns tense, emotions rise, bodies stiffen, and a conversation goes from easy to difficult. Sensing the tension, one or both of the participants attempt to ease it. Gottman calls it "putting on the brakes" in the rising escalation. A repair attempt can be a joke, an apology, a statement of empathy and understanding—anything that communicates we are in this together. In a troubled marriage, these attempts at creating peace go unseen. The difference between peacemaking in a healthy marriage and a marriage soon to end in divorce is not the topic being discussed, the level of disagreement, or the ability to agree on the issue. The difference in part is a spouse's ability to recognize the offer of peace from their partner. Unhealthy couples do not see the attempt of their partner to deflate the tension in the conversation, so the partner feels rejected.

One aspect of being a peacemaker is always looking for opportunities to deflate tension and find common ground.

Tools of the Peacemaker

There is not a set formula for making peace. It's not a three-step process that can be accomplished with routine. Peacemaking is a personal process. It's more art than science. However, there are common tools every peacemaking couple can use.

The prerequisites for peacemaking are the other seven commitments, specifically mercy, understanding our need, meekness, and striving for something more than us. Mercy creates the safety necessary for the process of peacemaking, and recognizing our need gives us the humility to give and receive mercy. Meekness directs our actions in a balanced way, and striving for something bigger than us forces us to make peace in order to engage in the higher purpose of transformation.

The ability to submit to one another is a key tool for a peacemaking couple. If one person must always be right, always be followed, always be in charge, true peace will be difficult to find. If a couple can regularly submit to one another and submit personal desire to the well-being of the couple, peace will not be far behind.

There are places in which my wife is more informed, reasoned, and skilled to make a decision than I. Peace in those circumstances is easily found as I submit to her. In other areas, I'm more skilled, and she submits to me. As we submit to one another, trust is built, and the give-and-take of marriage is more easily navigated. Most of the mundane details of life fall into one of these categories in which one of us is better positioned to make a decision. Submitting to one another on a regular basis gives credibility to our opinions when we disagree. Disagreement is less likely to be a circumstance of trying to force our own way.

A peacemaker is often looking for a third way. Far too often, conflict is characterized by a false dichotomy. We are only presented with or only see two options, and we are forced to choose between the two. Kerry Patterson calls this the "sucker's choice."[10] Believing there are only two options causes people to quickly choose sides and fight for their choice. Far more often there is another option. The most common sucker's choice that couples make is to stay in a miserable marriage or to leave. Neither a bad marriage nor a divorce are what God intended. There is a third way—to improve the marriage.

The power of a third way is illustrated by William Ury, a Harvard Fellow who coauthored the classic *Getting to Yes*. He gave a TED talk[11] in which he told an ancient Middle East story of a father who left seventeen camels to his three sons. To the first he left half of the camels, to the second he left one-third of the camels, and to the youngest he left one-ninth of the camels. Since seventeen doesn't divide by two or three or nine, the brothers were at a standstill in their negotiations. Desperate, they sought out a wise old woman in their community to ask her advice. The woman considered their problem and told them that there was nothing she could say to assist them with this problem, but she did have one camel, and if they wanted it they could take it. They did, and then they had eighteen camels. The first son took his half (nine camels), the second son took his third (six camels), and the last son took his ninth (two camels). Nine plus six plus two equals seventeen, so they had one camel left over. They gave it back to the wise old woman.

Choices are rarely one or the other. Most often there are additional options that result in resolution and compromise, but they're more difficult to see. They require more work and are often overlooked by those who fail to understand the importance of peacemaking.

The most used tool of a peacemaker is common ground. In a world that makes war, that divides and conquers, most of us spot differences and begin there. A peacemaker is wise in identifying common ground and building on what is already shared. When we place differences or uncertainties within that context, the differences are minimized. When we begin with differences, we lose the context of the multiple issues we already agree on, and it can feel as though we disagree about everything. If we begin with common ground, any divide can seem reconcilable. Something as minor as beginning a serious conversation by restating our love for one another and our desire for our common good as a couple can radically change a difficult conversation.

Laughter is overlooked as a great tool for peacemaking. Laughing *at* your spouse doesn't build peace; however, joint laughter can be a wonderful way to build common ground, reorient a discussion back to what is important, and remind one another of the joy you share. The old marital advice is to remove all clothing when a discussion gets tense because nudity brings levity to any situation. Finding humor in every situation is a wonderful stress relief.

It is not often publicly discussed, but one of the funniest places is behind the scenes at a funeral home. While it's appalling for some to think about, a necessary part of coping with life is laughing even in the most serious moments. Without this laughter, the staff of a funeral home could probably not handle the stress of continual sorrow. The same is true for marriage. Laughter is nonnegotiable. It must happen. While some will laugh more than others, it seems as though the healthier a marriage, the more prevalent joint laughter is.

Peacemaking at Home

Some would assume if you can't make peace at home, where can you make it? The opposite might be true: if you can make peace at home, you can make it anywhere. It seems as though peacemaking at home would be easier—the home truly should be a laboratory to test and practice everything we are called to do. Yet sometimes it seems like the most difficult location to accomplish life's most important tasks. So much is involved, so much is exposed, and so much is seemingly on the line that it is often easier to make peace with a stranger than with your spouse. However, nowhere is peace more rewarding than at home. While the first steps of peacemaking are most difficult there, once the life of a peacemaker is embraced by a couple, it becomes a way of life. The earlier these initial steps are taken by a couple, the more rewarding marriage becomes.

Without a doubt, couples who continually make peace with one another are lucky. They know and are known by their spouse. They are not surprised by conflict or fearful that the normal disagreements in life might hurt their relationship. They do not take things as personally as others. They can separate their lasting love from a temporary confrontation. They are quick to get help because they know many issues cannot be solved without an outside perspective. They can live with disagreement and differing opinions because they trust one another. They feel wholly involved in their marriage because there are no off-limit topics or aspects of themselves they need to hide. They do not have to worry about every word they say for fear their spouse might be offended or hurt.

Unlike the Nobel Peace Prize, making peace in marriage doesn't come with recognition, a medal, or a cash prize, but it can often be just as challenging as any negotiated settlement a political leader has achieved. While the process of making peace is difficult, the reward is well worth the struggle.

BE INTENTIONAL

1. Which of the three types of counterfeit peace is most present in your relationship?
2. Which is one of the tools of a peacemaker you can use more often? Why?
3. What's the most common stone you use against your spouse? How can you drop that stone and plant a seed?
4. What prevents us from doing the work of making peace?

COMMITMENT 8

HAPPILY ENDURE WHATEVER MAY COME

It's not unusual for me to wake up via text message. I'm a night owl, so while I stay up later than most, I'm not early to rise. Many people start their day before my kids come bounding down the stairs and wake me up. But this text message was a little earlier than usual. "I think you just offended a lot of really obsessed strong people," it read. At first I had no idea what my friend was talking about. Then I remembered—this was the day that my article about adultery was published. I wrote the article through the lens of an exercise problem, and my headline used the name of the most popular program in my community—CrossFit.[1]

This article is one I write at least once a year. I frame it differently each time, but on an annual basis I write a basic article about boundaries that would protect couples from engaging in an affair. They are basic commonsense ideas that every marriage counselor and writer promotes every day. And every time I write the article, I get a passionate response in reply.

Minutes after the CrossFit article posted, I received text messages warning me of the anger. By the time I got to the office, my voice mail was blinking and my social media notifications were going crazy. I was called stupid, closed-minded, old-fashioned, prudish, and too religious. While I understood some people might not like me using one exercise program as an example, the vicious response to the article itself was shocking. I couldn't figure it out, so I called a friend to help me understand. He said, "People are just mad you wrote this in response to the affairs that just occurred at our local Box." I laughed out loud. I didn't know they had just had a string of affairs at the local gym.

The irony of the response is that one would think a group of people who had just seen the devastating effects of multiple affairs would cheer an article that compliments their program while also providing basic guardrails that would keep the affairs from happening again. Instead, many people lashed out.

It's an often overlooked characteristic of marriage—not everyone is for you. Some knowingly oppose you. Others do so without conscious intent. Even your own brokenness will fight against what you desire. When you as a couple are ignorant regarding opposition to your marriage, you can unknowingly be hindered by the hardship. Yet when you recognize that the pursuit of good is often met with opposition, even that opposition can be used to strengthen your relationship. If you are doing right, some will hate, revile, and attack you. Even in the small decisions of everyday life in which you try to honor God, love your spouse, and create good families, you will have opposition.

Marriage thrives when a couple recognizes hardship, embraces it, and uses every situation and circumstance as an opportunity to recommit to one another, learn new skills, and grow both individually and as a couple.

When Others Criticize Your Marriage

If you are doing marriage right, others will criticize you. Some will laugh. Some will mock. A few will seriously critique. They will not like your decisions, be confused by your quirks, and judge many of your actions as unnecessary or harmful. The absence of criticism isn't a sign of health; it's a warning sign of disease. I would be concerned if no one ever laughed at how you do marriage. And I would be concerned if a good number of people don't find you somewhat odd.

There are two basic reasons that others criticize good relationships. First, the average person doesn't know what it takes to make marriage work. We live in a culture of brokenness. In few places is this seen more than in marriage. While divorce may not be as rampant as some think (don't believe it when they say half of all marriages end in divorce), it's far more prevalent than it should be. We have neither been taught nor learned what it takes to make marriage work. Because of this ignorance, we can applaud bad behavior and critique good behavior in others. Without knowing it, we can hurt the relationships of others because we are giving advice (and judgment) from a position of ignorance.

We invent our own scenarios of how to experience success in marriage.

Sadly, most of what we think would make marriage succeed actually makes it fail. Consider living together before marriage. It makes total sense that living together prior to committing to one another would lead to a better marriage. (How could a test drive make it less likely that we would enjoy the car?) However, study after study has shown that living together lessens the bonds of marriage and increases the likelihood of divorce. Many attitudes and actions that people assume are commonsense approaches to a successful marriage will actually prevent healthy marriages from occurring. The truth is often contrarian.

Second, a person naturally tries to justify their mistakes by criticizing others. Even if they know what is right, they are likely to critique others to justify past mistakes. Sometimes our loudest critics are those who have never experienced any success in relationships. Their criticism is often a form of self-defense. They are trying to deflect attention from their failures by attacking relationships that are working. I often tell couples as they are recovering from affairs that their loudest critics will be guilty of something very similar or far worse. I encourage them to respond kindly and give it time. Eventually it comes to light that the critic was trying to bring the couple down to make themselves feel better.

If we're living right, many people will say we're living wrong. It should actually concern us if no one is criticizing us. While we can't blindly assume every criticism is a sign we are right, we also shouldn't assume any presence of criticism necessarily means we are doing something wrong.

What They Critique

Outsiders will criticize a variety of aspects of a healthy marriage. The most common critiques are about:

- *Effort*. Society often believes a good marriage takes little effort. They think it comes naturally. You know better. Others will laugh at the effort you put into marriage if you are doing it right. They will think you work too hard, think too much, and are overly concerned with protecting yourself and your relationship.
- *Decisions*. No matter what you decide, others will critique it. Because they don't know the whole story, don't have all the information, and didn't experience the pressure of making the choice, they will assume what you have decided is wrong.
- *Boundaries*. Few people understand the true threat of infidelity. Healthy couples are aware of the threat and set firm boundaries to protect themselves and others. If there is nothing that others roll their eyes at or think you've gone overboard about when it comes to setting boundaries with those of the opposite sex, you are probably setting yourself up for failure.
- *Time*. A good relationship demands a quantity of quality time. Because others don't always know what a good marriage requires, proper allocation of time seems foreign to them. They may mock you when you choose not to go out with friends or can't attend a game. When you put family first, others won't understand.
- *Fidelity*. In a world of broken promises, staying true to your word seems weird. Many feel as though the heart

can't be controlled and our passions choose whatever they wish. Those who believe this will have a tough time understanding those who desire to uphold their wedding vows. Sometimes when others call you old-fashioned, that's a great compliment.

- *Health.* When all someone has experienced is a bad relationship, they can quickly write the story that all marriages are like that. If you have a good marriage, others will critique it as too good to be true. They will think it is a charade. While no marriage is perfect, many marriages are very good, and that is hard for some people to understand.

- *Marriage.* Some will simply criticize the concept of marriage. They might believe it's outdated or no longer necessary. They won't understand the necessity for a legal document or the hassle of a public commitment. Many see marriage as restrictive and a hindrance to love or freedom. What they fail to realize is that love and freedom flourish in the midst of true commitment.

Critical Response

We must be very careful in how we respond to criticism of our relationships. It could be that people who deeply love us truly see a problem and are attempting to help us. But others speak not from true concern but from ignorance or an attempt to make themselves feel better.

Our challenge is to recognize the difference. In some areas, we should be so confident it doesn't matter what anyone says. We should form a plan and not be moved from our choices of love, devotion, compassion, discipline, and the pursuit of the best marriage possible. In other areas, we must always be humble and willing to consider the possibility the other person is right. We should check our own actions and attitudes to see if we can make better choices.

How to Protect Your Marriage

They should laugh at you. They should talk behind your back. They should doubt the strength of your marriage. In a society where marriages are falling apart, where affairs happen every day, where a healthy marriage seems like a strange marriage, you should take steps to protect your marriage that other people find odd, offensive, and even laughable.

Imagine an American soldier hiking through the mountains in Afghanistan—helmet on his head, in full uniform, finger near the trigger of his weapon. Now imagine that same soldier dressed that way and walking in the same manner down the aisle of the local Walmart. We would think he is suffering from PTSD. He would need help. In the same way, if he hiked through the mountains of Afghanistan in his gym shorts and an American T-shirt, we would think he was insane. There is no need to dress for war in the midst of peace, and it is unwise to dress for peace in the midst of war.

As I look at many married couples, I see far too many dressed for war at home and dressed for peace outside of the home. It should be reversed. Home should be a place of peace. It should be the place for ultimate security. In the climate of love, forgiveness, and mercy, couples should be willing to let their guard down. Yet many are so wounded, they walk into their houses with helmet on, in uniform, and with their finger near the trigger. They constantly scan the horizon for danger and are quick to fight even when they aren't in danger. At the same time, they take off the fatigues when they leave their house. Their guard is down at work. They aren't looking for danger at a restaurant. They are unaware they are under attack. They are sitting ducks in a war being waged for the soul of their marriage.

In order to protect our marriage, we need to dress for peace at home and dress for war everywhere else.

Dress for peace at home by doing the following:

- Be quick to listen.
- Be quick to share a feeling before a fact.
- Seek conversation.
- Seek service.
- Seek any opportunity to show you are on your spouse's team.
- Develop a healthy sex life.

Dress for war outside the home by doing the following:

- Understand the danger.
- Beware of giving or receiving false signals.
- Never speak negatively of your spouse before someone of the opposite sex.
- Do not listen to those of the opposite sex speaking negatively about their spouse.
- Never flirt.
- Don't showcase your personality for others; save it for home.

It's easy for couples to forget there is a war for their marriage. As a pastor, I'm reminded of it every day. Rarely does twenty-four hours pass in which I'm not dealing with some casualty of war. It happens primarily from apathy and ignorance. Few couples seek to destroy their marriage; instead, they let it slowly decay over time. They walk unaware through a battlefield, and it's only a matter of time before they suffer loss.

In a world where a bad marriage is so normal, couples must act in unusual ways so they don't suffer the same fate. Those ignorant of the battle will not understand. They will laugh, mock, and question. They will claim you are a religious nut or overly paranoid. They will ridicule you to justify themselves. Living in a sin-soaked world, you must take certain actions for the sake of righteousness that others will not understand. When they mock or revile you or misunderstand your intentions, do not be discouraged. It is a sign you are taking your marriage seriously.

Internal Sabotage

It may not surprise us that some outside of our marriage will attempt to sabotage what we are trying to accomplish. But the threats to our marriage aren't only external. There are also internal threats we have to be willing to recognize and endure.

When meeting with a couple in the weeks before their wedding, I often ask them, "What are some things from each of your families that you want to replicate in your new family, and what are some things you don't want to emulate?" In nearly every case, the couple can point to aspects of both families that they appreciate and a few things that are either unhealthy or they just want a different path for. I always warn the couple that they shouldn't be surprised if some in their family are hurt and defensive when they choose a different way. Either to justify their decisions or to try to convince the couple that the family—not the couple—is right, extended family members can overinvolve themselves in the decision-making process. Instead of accepting the rights of the new couple to form their family however they wish, the extended family will pressure, judge, and try to manipulate the couple. For a successful marriage, the couple must be able to respectfully choose a different way from their families of origin. Without being judgmental toward their families or acting like they are better than them, the couple must make their own decisions and be willing to live with them.

While extended family can be a challenge, the toughest difficulties will come when couples unknowingly sabotage themselves. In every marriage, there will be times in which our spouse is wrong and they will be tempting us to make bad decisions. Likewise, there will be moments in which we are wrong and we will be tempting them to make bad decisions. In these moments, we must choose what is right no matter what our spouse believes.

One of the great gifts of marriage is also one of its great difficulties. In a loving relationship, we have someone close to us who has the right and the responsibility to tell us no. They are expected to hold us accountable and to assist us in making good decisions. This is great in theory but difficult in practice. No one likes to be told no, and the closer someone is to us, the more difficult the disagreement can be.

While our vows should take precedence over personal preferences, opinions, and morally neutral decisions, they do not trump right or wrong. Just because it's our spouse who is trying to talk us into immoral behavior doesn't make the behavior acceptable. Some of the opposition we will face when trying to do right is from the very one who is supposed to be helping us make the best decisions. We must be willing to love them even as we refuse to do what they say.

A couple must show great discernment in this area. While we should never allow our spouse to talk us into bad behavior, we must be careful not to ordain our personal preferences as being morally superior to other options. If your wife desires to make a purchase that you consider a waste of money, those are differing opinions, not necessarily moral questions. However, if she wants you to cover up her embezzlement of money, that is a clear issue of morality. With the first, you might disagree, but your wife is free to make whatever decision she wants, and you may choose to help in whatever way you can. With the second, you disagree, beg your wife not to make a bad decision, and will not play a part in assisting her in the process. While we can expect occasional moments in which a spouse might tempt us to do wrong, we have to be very careful not to assume every time we disagree that we are morally right and they are morally wrong.

In a healthy relationship, spouses view one another as a partner regarding the big issues of life. While it might be uncomfortable to tell a spouse no, it is a great gift. Rare would be the case in which my wife told me not to do something and I chose to do it anyway. I would have to be completely convinced that the decision before me was of extreme importance and my actions were clearly right. In nearly every case, if my wife says no, then I trust her judgment and will not move forward.

Not all opposition is external. There will be times in which those who love us most—even ourselves—will try to convince us to do the wrong thing. We must humbly but strongly choose what is right.

Boundaries

The boundary someone is most tempted to ignore is the one they most need to observe.

Every marriage needs firm guardrails to protect it. Without specific plans, clear boundaries, and general operating procedures, an individual leaves themselves open to a significant moral failure that will either greatly hinder the relationship or completely destroy it.

There are no exceptions. It's not a guy issue or something a few people need to consider. It is a universal rule—every married person needs physical and emotional boundaries with people of the opposite sex. Whenever a couple says "I do" to one another, they are also saying "I won't" to everyone else. A foolish person simply hopes they will have the willpower to withstand every temptation that comes their way. A wise person knows their willpower is limited and puts boundaries in place to lessen the number of temptations they face so that their strength is in full supply when they do face them.

Happily married people have firm guardrails and stick to them. The greatest threat to a marriage is the moment a spouse is tempted to ignore a normally respected boundary.

Let's say your spouse has open access to your text messages, but there is one message you decide to delete. You never have a meal with a person of the opposite sex, but this one time you want to make an exception. You never lie to your spouse about where you are or who you are with, but on this occasion you are tempted to do so. Wisdom creates boundaries, but it also lives by them. The moment you are tempted to violate a normally held boundary with a person of the opposite sex, you should recognize the temptation, withstand it, and be on guard with that person.

Danger lies not in the place where we think there is the most temptation, but in the place where we are most likely to let down our guard. Physical and emotional affairs have far less to do with a specific person and far more to do with foolish decision making and putting ourselves in places where we are likely to succumb to temptation.

Guardrails only work if they are lived by consistently and with great diligence. Our hearts are so deceptive that if we ever let down our guard, we will do so with the person or in the situation where we most need our guard up.

With all the couples I have seen go through the chaos of an affair, I've never had a single person tell me, "I always knew I would do this." Rare is the case in which a person plans on having an affair. Who in their right mind would cause such pain to their spouse, family, and community? People do not have affairs in their right mind. They do so out of deception. They are lured into adultery and make poor decisions without any consideration of the real consequences. What begins as a minor bending of normal rules or a simple exception to the usual operating procedures can lead to the destruction of one's family, reputation, and life.

Show me the place or the person you are not being diligent with in your thoughts, actions, or attitudes, and I'll show you the place or the person that is the greatest threat to your marriage. Talk with your spouse about which boundaries you both will live by as a couple, and then live by them.

> **PRACTICING THE COMMITMENT** A healthy marriage requires a good offense and defense. Every couple needs to create healthy boundaries they will not cross in order to create a good defense to protect their relationship. They also need to engage in healthy habits to strengthen their relationship and diminish the influence of temptation. List ten boundaries that others might consider overboard but that you and your spouse will live by to protect yourself, honor each other, and not give the wrong impression to others. (For example, we won't eat alone with a person of the opposite sex, we won't ride alone in a car with a person of the opposite sex, we will share passwords on social media accounts.) After developing the boundaries, reevaluate a month later to see if the rules are useful.

Whatever May Come

Husband and wife should have a single mindset—"Whatever comes our way we will tackle together." Healthy couples happily endure whatever may come, yet they don't confuse endurance for apathy or settling or denial.

On nearly a weekly basis, I meet with couples whose marriages are in shambles. Many of them believe my goal is to keep them from a divorce. It's not. While I hope they don't divorce, I have a much greater desire for them—that they'll have the best marriage they possibly can. Perfection is not the goal. Struggles will always be present. But simply hoping not to divorce is not an outcome worth pursuing.

Many couples wrongly settle for whatever may come. A husband cheats and gets caught, but nothing really changes. A wife's heart slowly dies, but no effort is expended to bring it back to life. While it's right that we mourn the things in our relationship that are not what we desire, we should not just resign ourselves to second-rate relationships. Instead, we should see endurance as an attitude of work. When challenges present themselves, we will do everything necessary to overcome them. While others live in denial, pretending as though nothing is wrong, we will accept the hardships and find ways to use them to our advantage. This demands something from us—a willingness to live for our spouse.

Can You Live for Your Spouse?

It's a common question I ask young men as they contemplate marriage: "Are you willing to die for her?" It's not an exaggerated question. Until a man and woman are willing to give their lives for one another, they have no business getting married. That's what a wedding is—a public announcement made to God, one another, and society that a couple is willing to sacrifice themselves for one another. When a man and woman say "I do," they are promising to put the other person before their own happiness. They are promising to sacrifice their own selves for the well-being of the other. They are vowing to die for each other.

In a wedding ceremony, I try to remind the couple that this acceptance of death might come in a dramatic form. It's possible that while on their honeymoon, the couple could walk into a convenience store where someone pulls a gun. In that moment, the groom has vowed he is willing to lay down his life for his bride. Yet far more likely than that one dramatic act, marriage requires that the couple die to themselves on a daily basis. Time and time again over their life span, they must be willing to die to their need to get the last word, have their way, win the fight, and make their point.

A good marriage is built through a thousand small acts. As a husband and wife lay down their lives for one another, the marriage thrives.

Being willing to die for one another is vital for a healthy marriage, but it doesn't stop there. While every potential spouse needs to be asked, "Are you willing to die for your spouse?" there is a second question that needs to be asked: "Are you willing to live for your spouse?"

It's not enough to restrain ourselves on behalf of our spouse. Love must also motivate us to action.

While our spouse should never be the primary reason for our existence—God plays that role—we should live our lives, in part, for one another. My love for my wife should inspire me toward life. Who wants to be married to someone who isn't full of life? Sometimes there are situations and seasons in which our spouse will not be vibrant or full of life. Yet in most cases, marriage should be the intersection of two people who are full of life, light, and joy. Failing to live our lives to the fullest is not just a dereliction of duty to God; it's also a failure of living up to our wedding vows.

In order to live for my spouse, I will:

- *Seek to contribute to the betterment of society.* God has given me talents, abilities, and desires that are best expressed when trying to assist others. I will seek to use what I have to make life better for those around me, including my spouse.

- *Continue to learn, grow, and achieve.* If we aren't changing, we are dying. For as long as God gives me breath, I will seek to better understand myself, learn new skills, become a better man, and attempt to achieve things.

- *Work on my own happiness and sense of self.* My wife is not in charge of my happiness or my self-worth. We are both to bring happiness into marriage rather than demanding that our marriage make us happy. My identity is found in who God created me to be and what he has said about me. I will not expect my wife to give to me what can only be received from God.

- *Live in reality and not avoid feelings.* Life is full of joys and sorrows. It has many ups and downs. For me to live life, I have to engage in reality. I have to admit pain and accept heartache while not allowing those hurts to hinder my ability to laugh and love. Stoicism is not living. Denial is not life. To live means I won't pretend things are one way when they are actually something else. I will laugh and cry. And I will welcome my wife into those moments of life.

- *Find my purpose in God.* Humanity was created with a purpose. Until we understand our place in this world—as a supporting character, not the central figure—we can't experience life to its fullest. In part for my wife, I will seek a relationship with God so I can better understand who I am and what I am to do in life.

Marriage begins when two people are willing to die for each other, but it flourishes as they learn to live for each other.

The Luck of Adversity

How can opposition, criticism, and even persecution be a blessing? How can they be used not only for God's glory but also for our good?

One of the fascinating things about being a pastor is that I interact with a variety of people going through very similar situations. While no circumstance is identical, the general stories of our lives are not very unique. Illness, grief, death, and opposition all have common themes.

Allison and Michelle were diagnosed in the same month. While the masses were in different places, the general treatment and prognosis were about the same. Both were malignant tumors that were caught early. Both would likely have very successful outcomes. But both women would have to endure months of difficult treatment—chemo and radiation.

Looking back on the experience, Michelle and her husband consider those months some of the most meaningful ones of their marriage. With tears in their eyes, they explain to other couples how difficult the days were, but with a deep joy they describe how the experience gave them a greater appreciation for life, each other, and the days that they have remaining.

Allison tells a different story. Within weeks of her being diagnosed, her husband left. He wasn't willing to walk beside her during her darkest days. He thought he had suffered enough in the marriage and wasn't willing to endure anymore. What Michelle would describe as a marriage-strengthening season, Allison would define as the event that ended her marriage. Two relationships, similar diagnoses, with radically different outcomes.

Opposition, hardship, and even persecution can be a blessing to a marriage because they can cause a husband and wife to cling to each other to endure. As they walk side by side through the sorrow, they learn more about each other and themselves. They grow in trust and understanding. Even though more flaws are revealed, they also see a more meaningful aspect of one another. While they weep over the experience, they rejoice in the deeper levels of intimacy and love.

But what drives some couples together drives others apart. Maybe it's just revealing a divide that has always been there. In some cases it just precipitates what would have happened anyway. No matter the circumstance, it's very sad. When faced with an opportunity that, while difficult, could greatly influence their relationship for good, some people run.

Persecution will not be good for every marriage. There is a reason it's the last of the Beatitudes. Without the previous seven commitments, opposition might drive a marriage apart. However, when a couple recognizes their own poverty of spirit and mourns that condition, when they meekly pursue a righteousness they can never fully find, when they purify their hearts and the heart of the relationship, when they freely give and receive mercy, and when they find a way to make peace, then anything—even persecution—can be seen as a blessing because it will make their marriage stronger.

BE INTENTIONAL

1. What are some boundaries you have created in your marriage that others criticize but you know help your relationship?

2. How do you know the difference between criticism you should ignore and criticism you should consider?

3. What do you believe is the greatest threat to your marriage? What guardrails have you created to protect yourself?

4. What is your game plan for when difficult times hit? Who will help you through those times?

CONCLUSION

Every year at Christmas as the church is decorated for the holiday season, there is an uptick in funerals. I'm not sure why it happens—maybe it's the change in weather or the added stress of the holidays. Maybe it's just coincidence and funerals seem more commonplace when they really aren't. Whatever the case, nearly every Christmas season I stand before several widows or widowers as their spouse lies in a casket between us. In those moments, an outsider would look at the horrific grief of a husband or wife and say they are anything but fortunate. There might be a greater sorrow than losing a spouse, but there aren't many. I've looked into the eyes of far too many men and women. The loss, confusion, uncertainty, and pain can be overwhelming.

In the moments before the service or after the service when everyone has left and it's just me and the family standing near the casket, I hear some common phrases:

- "I don't know what I'm going to do without him."
- "Isn't she pretty?"
- "She was so good to me."

- "I'm going to miss his grin."
- "I don't remember life without her."

But do you know the most common line I hear, standing beside a casket of someone who had a long, happy marriage? "We were so lucky." A marriage that lasts a lifetime feels like the greatest stroke of luck. In part, it is good fortune. Many people never have the chance for a long marriage—war or illness or an accident can rob a couple of the chance of a lifetime romance. Many others desire that kind of love, but personal choices or the choices of others have prevented their relationships from lasting.

Those who are fortunate to find someone to love and navigate with through life's demands to experience a meaningful, loving marriage that lasts for many years—they truly are the lucky ones. While their luck is not devoid of hard work, their effort doesn't seem to match the outcome; it seems to pale in comparison to the tremendous blessing of true love.

When we embrace the eight commitments, marriage can become a lifelong blessing. The commitments are contrarian. They aren't what we expect. Ask someone what it takes to have a happy marriage, and they would never say that we should mourn the inadequacies of ourselves and the institution of marriage. We don't naturally understand that it's in our weaknesses and not our strengths that marriage can thrive. Each commitment is alien to us. Yet each one should be embraced. What comes naturally to us does not work. We are surrounded by the brokenness of people acting in ways that seem right to them. While the choices make sense, the outcomes are not what they expect. Humanity needs a better way. And we have one.

If the way that seems natural to us does not give us the outcome we desire, we must submit to another way. The eight commitments found in this book are the other way. They are the way of Jesus.

A few thousand years ago on a Galilean hillside, a seemingly insignificant carpenter from a little-known town began one of the most famous speeches ever given by announcing the blessedness, the good fortune, the luck of a group of people who seemed so unlucky. It was horrible news for some in the crowd who believed life was set to their advantage because of position or power or intellectual ability or tradition. Jesus destroyed their self-confidence by announcing good fortune to a group of people who seemed worthy of pity instead of envy.

In the Sermon on the Mount, Jesus described the ethic that defines his kingdom. As a king, he has sovereign rule and is free to determine which values and actions will be praised. Much like a political party constructs a platform or a nation drafts a constitution, the kingdom of heaven has a defined way of life. Jesus described that life in his famous sermon.

The introduction to the Sermon on the Mount sets the stage for how different God's values are from ours. He begins with eight "blessed" statements.[1] The word *blessed* has been translated many ways. Because of its Latin connection, some would translate it as "happy." "Lucky" is another option.

Jesus says, "These are the lucky ones," yet what he lists do not seem to be lucky: the poor in spirit, mourners, the meek, those who hunger and thirst, the merciful, the pure in heart, the peacemakers, and those who are persecuted.

It seems like these are the people to be pitied, to be avoided, yet Jesus says they are the lucky ones. They are the ones who have a leg up with God. They are the ones more likely to experience a relationship with God. They are the ones envied in God's kingdom.

We see a striking contrast to our world:

- In a world that envies the rich, God values the poor in spirit.
- In a world that is obsessed with strength, God highlights meekness.
- In a world that assumes God raises up those who are full of righteousness, he speaks of those who do not have it but want it.
- In a world that values revenge, God values mercy.
- In a world that values ability, God values purity of heart.
- In a world that values winners, God values peacemakers.
- In a world that values the powerful, God values the persecuted.

We can't miss the news in this announcement. By saying who is "lucky" in God's eyes, Jesus was also saying who was unlucky. The strong, powerful, confident, have-it-all-together people who were intrigued by Jesus were probably put off by his words. Those who trusted in themselves and their ability probably walked away at this moment.

This was horrible news for some that day. For those who were bursting with righteousness, Jesus announced they were in trouble. For those who thought of themselves as rich and deserving, Jesus announced they were out of luck.

This is horrible news for some in our day. If people think they deserve God, if they think he owes them, if they think they have earned his love, if they are proud of their abilities and accomplishments before God—there seems to be no place for them in his kingdom. If their spiritual plan is to one day stand before God and say, "Look at how much I did for you," Jesus seems to communicate in the Beatitudes that they are out of luck.

While this is bad news for some, it is tremendously good news for others. God's kingdom values people this world rejects—the least expected, the least deserving. The ones pitied in this world are envied in God's kingdom. The ones who seem out of luck in this world are the lucky ones in God's kingdom. The ones this world might call cursed, Jesus calls blessed.

Marriage was God's idea. Before sin, before the chaos of the fall, and in the midst of perfection, God said it is not good for humans to be alone. He created men and women to be together, knowing this relationship would be complicated after the fall. The original differences that complemented one another would irritate each other as pride came into the equation. While sin marred God's design, it did not change the importance of marriage.

Trusting God's sovereignty, we can easily say God designed marriage knowing humanity would fall in order to use it as an avenue through which he would reveal to us our need for redemption and offer to us a playground where we could work out our salvation with fear and trembling. Nothing reveals the sinfulness of humanity as much as marriage; nowhere are the effects of the gospel more powerfully communicated than within marriage.

God's intent is for marriage to be a physical representation of his relationship with the church. The reconciliation he has made between himself and the church is to be symbolized as two sinful people individually experience God's grace and then extend that grace to one another. As God sanctifies our hearts, making them like his own, a common avenue through which transformation takes place is marriage.

Marriage is more than an aid to help us endure earth; it's a pathway to prepare us for heaven. In this truth lies a key to understanding how to make marriage better. If God created marriage and is using it to prepare us for life with him, what does he value? What are his general operating procedures? What is the ethic of God's kingdom?

The Beatitudes, which were a bold announcement of who is lucky in God's kingdom, can form a matrix through which a successful marriage can be experienced. If a good marriage feels like good fortune, what defines the lucky ones? Those who learn to live God's ethic in the midst of his design for marriage have a leg up—they are the lucky ones.

"Blessed are the poor in spirit," Jesus said, "for theirs is the kingdom of heaven" (Matt. 5:3). The kingdom of heaven—that is the great hope. The Beatitudes begin and end with the same words: "theirs is the kingdom of heaven." Each blessing in between describes a different aspect of heaven—comfort, satisfaction, mercy. Yet the words of Jesus are not simply a description of what is to come in the next life. For Jesus, although the kingdom will be in the future, aspects of it are available now.

Already / Not Yet

In Matthew 4 Jesus began his ministry by saying, "The Kingdom of Heaven is near." The kingdom of heaven has an already-and-not-yet quality about it.

The kingdom is already. Having our eyes opened in faith, we have submitted ourselves to the rule and reign of God. We have recognized his authority over this world and our lives. We have been made citizens of heaven, able to invest treasures there, and live by the norms of heaven even while we are on earth.

Yet the kingdom is also not yet. A day is coming when Jesus will wipe every tear away, but until then we still suffer, we still sin, we still experience the consequences of this fallen world. The kingdom of God is still not fully yet, so prayers can be denied, good intentions can have bad outcomes, and horrible tragedies can take place and go unexplained because we live in a fallen world.

While we can wait for the not yet, the already should give us great hope. There are ways we can experience God's kingdom on earth. We do not have to wait to experience aspects of heaven or to live the way we will in heaven—to be the people we will be.

While the Beatitudes list some of the characteristics of heaven, they also list the characteristics of the citizens of heaven. "Blessed are the poor in spirit . . . those who mourn . . . the meek . . . those who hunger and thirst for righteousness . . . the merciful . . . the pure in heart . . . the peacemakers . . . those who are persecuted because of righteousness," Jesus said (Matt. 5:3–10). These are the lucky ones in God's eyes; this is the ethic of God's kingdom. If this is how we will be in heaven, if this is how God invites us to live now, if God designed marriage and desires it to bring him glory, it only makes sense that these characteristics define a healthy marriage.

1. "Blessed are the poor in spirit." Understanding our spiritual bankruptcy before God, our complete inability

to save ourselves or others, we should attack the great enemy of a good marriage—pride. When we understand our need, it creates the climate in which we can learn and mature.

2. "Blessed are those who mourn." We are a fallen people living in a fallen world. As we make an emotional connection to our sin, we can experience the comfort God gives. Emotional denial prevents us from realizing the comfort God offers. Emotional denial within marriage prevents us from connecting with one another.

3. "Blessed are the meek." It is neither the weak nor the arrogant who are blessed. Never showing anger and raging over every issue are two sides of the same coin. Neither is a healthy expression of passion.

4. "Blessed are those who hunger and thirst for righteousness." Every couple will fight. Either we will fight together or we will fight each other. Having a common pursuit is vital for any marriage. We were created to strive toward godliness. Having tasted God's grace, we desire to live in response to what he has done for us. It is a hunger and thirst not for money, power, or fame but for righteousness that leads to blessing.

5. "Blessed are the merciful." Giving and receiving mercy is the climate in which marriage is supposed to be lived. Without mercy, we could never be loved or find anyone to love. With mercy, all things are possible.

6. "Blessed are the pure in heart." There is an enemy of marriage, and he attempts to attack the heart of it. We must guard our hearts if we are going to have any

chance to make it. Impurity will cloud our eyes, making it impossible to see each other or God.

7. "Blessed are the peacemakers." We live in a world that divides and conquers, but blessing comes to those who can unite and advance. Peacemaking is a major task for the bride and groom who want to have a happy marriage.

8. "Blessed are those who are persecuted because of righteousness." Success doesn't come easily. There is a tremendous cost for what is most important. As we live by a different ethic, we will rub others the wrong way and confuse them, and often they will feel judged because we have chosen differently. Sorrow is sure to come and regret is guaranteed when we guard our marriage above all things.

The order of these commitments is no accident. While each influences the other, there is a natural progression to how Jesus listed these attitudes. It all begins with humility. As we recognize our own need before God and embrace our poverty of spirit, we are pushed into action. Knowing our own need allows us to properly mourn not only our failures but also the inadequacies of our spouse as well as the fallible nature of a union between two broken people. As we grieve what isn't, we are also motivated to make things the best we can. This demands from us meekness. Avoiding both apathy and aggression empowers us to make changes—not just for ourselves but in the context of a higher calling. Ultimately, our relationships were meant to bring glory to God as we reflect aspects of his nature through our love for one another.

Even on a lesser scale, our marriage is about more than just us—it is influential on children, family, and society at large. Lest we become overwhelmed by the task before us, we are reminded of our need for mercy. We must receive it and give it. As we do, our hearts are purified, allowing us to put aside falsehood and embrace truth. And it's only when our hearts are in the process of purification that we can begin to do the hard work of making peace. In our pursuit of peace, we will face many challenges and even persecution. But we can endure the persecution and hardships because God is faithful.

These eight concepts reveal an attitude, which shows us the *how* of God's kingdom and can easily translate to the *how* of marriage. In a world fixated on the external, a good marriage begins on the inside.

Inside Out

The Beatitudes are an invitation to a different way of life. They're a request to abandon the natural responses and assumptions of life in order to live by a unique set of values. Living in this way changes everything, especially marriage.

Notice how the change takes place. The method of God is rarely the method we would use. We live in an outside-in world, but the kingdom of heaven is inside out. It comes first to the human heart and then makes itself known to the world.

It seeks out the small and seemingly insignificant.

It comes incognito to this world in the form of a tiny baby in a remote location.

It doesn't spread through mass communication but through a relationship of one person to another.

It doesn't come in a shout but in a whisper.

It doesn't first come to kings and rulers but to common men and women.

It's just as concerned with the humble choices of a mom as the powerful decisions of Congress.

It's just as focused on how we treat the powerless as how we treat the powerful.

The kingdom of God is inside out, more concerned with the heart than the appearance. So God changes us from the inside out. He purifies our heart long before he changes our appearance. He changes our attitudes before our actions. He changes our motivations before our outcomes. He works from within.

We live in an outside-in world, but we have been invited to become part of an inside-out kingdom. The question is, which will we choose?

Will we choose to talk about inside out but live by outside in?

Will we claim we are part of God's kingdom but then worry more about a presidential election than the condition of our own hearts?

Will we claim to focus on the heart but take great pains to put on an act of some false spiritual condition rather than being open about sin?

Will we claim to believe in a sovereign, powerful God, while at the same time ignoring and being blind to his activity in this world?

God is an inside-out God. We saw it in the garden when sin entered the world—he didn't destroy the world but instead walked through the garden looking for Adam and Eve.

We saw it in the choosing of Israel—God blessed an insignificant nation so it could be a blessing to others.

We saw it in the coming of Jesus—he came not as a king on a throne but as an infant submitted to his mother.

We saw it in the actions of Jesus—God didn't move the masses but invested in the twelve so they could change the world.

We saw it and even now see it through the church—God uses the small things of this world to change the hearts of men and women.

From Genesis to Revelation, God reveals his pattern—he works from the inside out. His design for the world is the same for marriage—to work inside out. To change a culture of brokenness, he works in one heart at a time, one relationship at a time. To change a relationship, he doesn't do dramatically outward things but makes subtle changes in our hearts.

So it is with a better marriage—it begins on the inside. The Beatitudes show us how. If *Friends, Partners, and Lovers* told us *what* to do in marriage, *Happily* shows us *how* to do marriage. These are the mindsets and attitudes that we must possess and act on to improve our relationships.

Anyone who has ever experienced a great marriage would say it's as close to heaven as they have ever been. No marriage is perfect and every marriage experiences great difficulty, but there are seasons of delight that no other thing on earth can give us. They are glimpses of heaven.

Jesus gave eight characteristics of heaven in the Beatitudes. They differ from what we would naturally expect or naturally do. They confront our sinfulness and invite us into a different way of life. These characteristics aren't just ways we *will* be; they are ways we *could* be. They aren't just suggestions for heaven; they are definitions of God's way for life both in heaven and on earth.

If God defines the ethic of heaven and made marriage to be a reflection of heaven, it only makes sense that these eight characteristics would define a healthy marriage.

Happily Ever After

One of the great privileges of routinely standing before a couple as they commit their earthly lives solely to one another is that I continually reflect on my own marriage. I don't pretend to have a perfect marriage, but I am grateful to have a good one. My hope as I watch a newlywed couple walk up the aisle and into their new life together is that their relationship would be the most meaningful earthly relationship they will ever have. I truly hope they are happily married.

As I watch them walk away, I'm hopeful but not delusional. I know many of the struggles they will face. I'm probably far more aware of how close the tough days are for them. But the words I pass on to them before they say "I do" are not glossy words meant just to be sentimental. They are true words meant to challenge them in the choices they will make. No matter the Scripture read or the exact words used, my message is always the same—love one another.

Normally it's the feeling of love that has led the couple to this moment, but that feeling will not get them through the days to come. Only the *actions* of love will do that. Those actions can be described with a lot of verbs—love, forgive, serve, submit, sacrifice, partner, strengthen, listen, talk, think. All those actions should be done not begrudgingly but happily. The couple should know that while the tasks are not easy, to choose rightly and act wisely is the best course of action. Just as a fast-food worker may not find great pleasure in the individual request of a single customer, they still do the task with a good attitude, knowing that doing so will in fact lead to the outcomes they want and produce a well-being of life.

I don't expect any marriage to be continually defined by happiness. Many moments will feel like anything but that. However, I do believe that marriage was meant to make our lives better as we continually love and serve one another. We can find happiness—not from each other but with one another.

BE INTENTIONAL

1. Why do we focus more on external change than internal change? Why is internal change more productive in the long run?

2. How does believing that marriage is designed by God give us a greater road map for experiencing a satisfying relationship?

3. Which of the Beatitudes stands out the most to you? Why?

4. What's one specific change you can make regarding your marriage that will make it better?

NOTES

Introduction: *More Than Luck*

1. Casey E. Copen, Kimberly Daniels, Jonathan Vespa, and William D. Mosher, "First Marriages in the United States: Data from the 2006–2010 National Survey of Family Growth," *National Health Statistics Reports*, March 22, 2012, https://www.cdc.gov/nchs/data/nhsr/nhsr049.pdf.

Commitment 5 Happily Refuse Power Struggles

1. Kerry Patterson, Joseph Grenny, Ron McMillan, and Al Switzler, *Crucial Conversations* (New York: McGraw-Hill, 2002), 96.

Commitment 6 Happily Live in Truth

1. Timothy Keller, *The Meaning of Marriage* (New York: Dutton, 2011), 165.

Commitment 7 Happily Make Peace

1. "The LORD God said, 'It is not good for the man to be alone. I will make a helper who is just right for him'" (Gen. 2:18 NLT).

2. I can't remember where this came from.

3. John Gottman, *The Seven Principles for Making Marriage Work* (New York: Crown, 1999), 149.

4. "My dear brothers and sisters: You must all be quick to listen, slow to speak, and slow to get angry. Human anger does not produce the righteousness God desires. . . . If you claim to be religious but don't control your tongue, you are fooling yourself, and your religion is worthless" (James 1:19–20, 26 NLT).

5. Gottman, *Seven Principles*, 130.

6. Jim Collins, *Good to Great* (New York: HarperCollins, 2001), 65.

7. Kerry Patterson, Joseph Grenny, Ron McMillan, and Al Switzler, *Crucial Confrontations* (New York: McGraw-Hill, 2005), 81.

8. This image is found in chapter 14 of Max Lucado, *The Applause of Heaven* (Dallas: Word, 1990).

9. Gottman, *Seven Principles*, 2.

10. Patterson, Grenny, McMillan, and Switzler, *Crucial Conversations*, 38.

11. William Ury, "The Walk from 'No' to 'Yes,'" Filmed October 2010 at TEDxMidwest, TED video, Ted.com/talks/William_ury/up-next.

Commitment 8 Happily Endure Whatever May Come

1. See Kevin A. Thompson, "Beware of the CrossFit Affair," *Kevin A. Thompson* (blog), April 19, 2015, www.kevinathompson.com/beware-of-the-crossfit-affair.

Conclusion

1. See Matthew 7–9. There are actually nine "blessed" statements, but the ninth seems to be an explanation of the eighth.

Kevin A. Thompson (MDiv, Beeson Divinity School) is lead pastor at Community Bible Church, a growing multisite church with four locations in western Arkansas. Every year he meets with nearly one hundred couples with a range of needs, from premarital counseling to navigating the most serious betrayals. A marriage and parenting conference speaker, he blogs at www.kevinathompson.com. He and his wife, Jenny, have two children and live in Fort Smith, Arkansas.

KEVINATHOMPSON.COM

VISIT KEVIN ONLINE FOR INSPIRING
AND INFORMATIVE BLOGS ABOUT

- » MARRIAGE
- » LEADERSHIP
- » PARENTING
- » FAITH
- » CURRENT EVENTS
- » AND MORE

f KevinAThompsonAR

🐦 KevinAThompson
📌 KevinThompson_
📷 Kevin_A_Thompson

g+ KevinAThompson
in KevinAThompson
▶ Kevin A Thompson

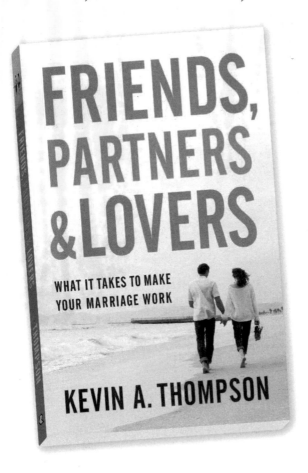